PATRIOTS DAY

The New England Patriots' March to the Super Bowl Championship

W9-BZB-555

BOSTON Herald

PATRIOTS DAY

The New England Patriots' March to the Super Bowl Championship

Sports Publishing, L.L.C.

Publisher: **Peter L. Bannon**

Senior Managing Editors: **Susan M. Moyer and Joseph J. Bannon Jr.**

Art Director: **K. Jeffrey Higgerson**

Graphic Designer: **Kenneth J. O'Brien**

Coordinating Editor: **Erin M. Linden-Levy**

Imaging: **Joseph T. Brumleve**

Boston Herald

President and Publisher: **Patrick J. Purcell**

Editor: **Andrew F. Costello**

Executive Sports Editor: **Mark Torpey**

Director of Photography: **Garo Lachinian**

Vice President/Promotion: **Gwen Gage**

Chief Librarian: **John Cronin**

Hard cover ISBN 1-58261-523-3

Soft cover ISBN 1-58261-521-7

SUPER BOWL XXXVI

PUBLISHER'S NOTE

Dear Friends:

The Patriots' magical Super Bowl season will go down as one of the great stories in the history of Boston. It's the kind of year fans will want to relive time and again for years to come.

In this book we give you the chance to do just that. Taken directly from the award-winning pages of the *Boston Herald* sports section, this volume documents every twist and turn on the way to the Pats' stunning victory over the heavily favored St. Louis Rams in Super Bowl XXXVI in New Orleans.

From the in-depth reporting of Michael Felger, to the bigger-than-life pictures from the *Herald's* photographers, to the witty headlines and stories provided by the *Herald's* sports staff, you'll see everything that went into making the Patriots champions of the world.

The Patriots were a team of destiny in 2001, but that's not to say everything went their way. The Pats overcame a host of off-field issues that would have broken apart weaker teams.

Quarterback coach Dick Rehbein died in training camp. Starting lineman Joe Andruzzi and his family of New York City firefighters had to endure the tragedies of Sept. 11. Franchise quarterback Drew Bledsoe nearly lost his life after taking a vicious hit along the sidelines in Week 2. Oft-troubled receiver Terry Glenn constantly taxed teammates and the coaching staff.

The Pats fought through all of it.

Behind the fresh-faced leadership of quarterback Tom Brady, the Pats' collection of unwanted veterans and unproven youngsters built momentum through the middle of the season before catching fire down the stretch run.

The Pats won six straight to close out the regular season and win the AFC East. Then came the memorable "Snow Bowl," in which the Pats came back in dramatic fashion to beat Oakland in the final game at Foxboro Stadium. Then came a stunning upset in Pittsburgh for the AFC Championship. Then came the shocker of all shockers: a three-point win over the heavily favored Rams in Super Bowl XXXVI.

The Patriots proved to everyone that team play, hard work and a belief in yourself can overcome any obstacle.

We are proud to present their story.

Patrick J. Purcell
Publisher

Sports

Izzy decides to make Sox' loss even worse
Page 100

Eerily familiar

Pats' opening-day loss, problems look a lot like last year **Story, Page 116**

DO OR DIE: Drew Bledsoe fights for yardage on a fourth-and-2 quarterback sneak late in yesterday's season-opener against the Bengals at Paul Brown Stadium. The ball was marked just short and the Pats went on to lose, 23-17. Complete coverage, Pages 119-124.

NFL SCOREBOARD

Sports

Banner race
Patriotism, records add to NYC Marathon
Page 66

ROOKIE JOE JOHNSON has emerged as a viable third-option in the Celtics' offense.

Bruins..........D6-54
College..........D4
Lotteries..........7
Schools..........6567-C7
Racing..........55, 65

New kids on the block

D-Backs end NY reign, win classic World Series
Story, Page 98

Patriots catch fire
Patriots receiver Troy Brown is mobbed by David Patten after catching a deflected pass and running it in for a touchdown in the third quarter of yesterday's 24-10 victory over the Falcons. Coverage, Pages 129-130.

Sports

Huskies have bite
Gibson stops 38 shots as NU atop BU
Page 72

DUKE BECOMES THE FINAL
Dix. 1 team to suffer a loss as Florida State beats the No. 1 Blue Devils. Page 71

Celtics..........75
Colleges..........73, 74
Colleges..........72
Lotteries..........56
Golf..........54

Bye and large!

Patriots win division, earn No. 2 seed with rout of Panthers **Story, Page 92**

KICKING INTO HIGH GEAR: Troy Brown leaves the pack behind as he races for the end zone with a 68-yard punt return during the third quarter for the Patriots' 38-6 victory over the Carolina Panthers in Charlotte, N.C., yesterday. Complete coverage, Pages 95-78.

NFL PLAYOFFS

Jets kicker John Hall (left) gets his due after his 53-yard field goal beat the Raiders.

AFC PLAYOFFS
First-round byes...

NFL Roundup Pages 56, 59

Two for the road
THE BRUINS take advantage of the weary Islanders, skating to a 4-2 win on Long Island.

BRIAN ROLSTON gets the call from Team USA, enabling him to join the Olympic squad for the second time in his career.
Page B10

SUNDAY Sports

New direction
Lappas, UMass are enjoying fresh start
Pages B20, B21

PULLOUT SECTION • DECEMBER 23, 2001 • BOSTON SUNDAY HERALD

Sports

End is near
Another loss, another step closer for Sox
Page 108

BOSTON RED SOX

BRUINS DEFENSEMAN
Nick Boynton is hoping to...

Black and Drew

Bledsoe, Patriots roughed up by Jets in home-opening loss **Story, Page 132**

NFL SCOREBOARD

Indy's Terrence Wilkins takes a punt back for a TD.

COLTS..........16
JETS..........10
PANTHERS..........
VIKINGS..........
PACKERS..........
BEARS..........
BUCCANEERS..........
COWBOYS..........
RAIDERS..........
CHIEFS..........
RAMS..........
SEAHAWKS..........
BROWNS..........
JAGUARS..........
SAINTS..........
FALCONS..........
TITANS..........

PICKED OFF: Patriots quarterback Drew Bledsoe leaves the field in frustration after throwing a third-quarter interception during yesterday's 10-3 loss to the New York Jets at Foxboro Stadium. Bledsoe was taken to Mass. General Hospital following the game.

Sports

Everett on outs
Source: Carl still wants a trade from Sox
Page 90

KENNY WALLS SCORES 21
as BC beats BU, 82-65, in the first game between the teams in 20 years. Page 78

Bruins..........88
Celtics..........89
College football..........82-83
Colleges..........76
Lotteries..........68

A notch below

Mistake-prone Patriots can't match up to NFL-best Rams **Story, Page 108**

McCLEON
21

NFL SCOREBOARD

Jets QB Curtis Martin breaks through to win over Indianapolis.

49ERS..........
SAINTS..........
BENGALS..........
RAIDERS..........
COLTS..........
JAGUARS..........
FALCONS..........
EAGLES..........
CARDINALS..........
TITANS..........
BRONCOS..........
BROWNS..........
GIANTS..........
BILLS..........
49ERS..........
PANTHERS..........
STEELERS..........
JAGUARS..........
CHIEFS..........
CHARGERS..........
BRONCOS..........
CARDINALS..........

PICKED APART: Patriots quarterback Tom Brady hears it from Rams defenders Aeneas Williams (left) and Dexter McCleon after throwing a 24-27 loss at Foxboro Stadium.

Sports

BC: New Heights
Eagles aiming for Top 10 after latest victory
Page 78

JOHN BUZ' DRAW WITH
Coyote Holyfield has shut-drawn some heavy criticism. Kimball, Page 80

Celtics..........65, 66
Bruins..........62
College..........80-73
Lotteries..........52
Racing..........62, 60

Pats get leg up

Receive the breaks and the kicks in OT win over Bills **Story, Page 100**

VINATIERI
4

NFL SCOREBOARD

NFL Roundup Pages 68, 69

WHAT A KICK: Patriots players had Adam Vinatieri's overtime field goal (above) and return Mike Carey's controversial ruling right) to thank for yesterday's 13-0 victory over the Bills — a result that left Buffalo less Clemons (bottom right) less than satisfied.

SUNDAY Sports

BOSTON HERALD

Grilled Tuna
Kraft holds all the aces in Jets deal

D-day in...

GHOST BUSTERS

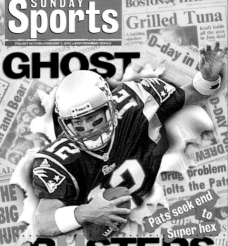

THE BIG HURT

Drug problem jolts the Pats

Pats seek end to Super hex

PULLOUT SECTION • FEBRUARY 3, 2002 • BOSTON SUNDAY HERALD

Sports

to 2-0 lead
Story, Page 90

to tie Blackhawks
Page 82

Falling to earth

Brady throws four interceptions as Patriots lose in Denver **Story, Page 108**

NFL SCOREBOARD

Buffalo's Rob Johnson heads off San Diego's Gerald Dixon.

SEEN THERE, DONE THAT: Patriots quarterback Tom Brady gets a pat on the helmet from Drew Bledsoe after throwing his fourth and final interception late in yesterday's 31-20 loss to the Broncos at Invesco Field in Denver.

NFL Roundup Pages 56, 67

Sports

Rocket's turn
Clemens, NY hope to keep Mariners quiet
Page 86

D'backs rule NL
Arizona wraps up Atlanta to make first World Series
Page 80

Pats hit it big

■ Patten, Brady lead a special team effort **Story, Page 104**
■ QB's not some one-game wonder **Mazz, Page 102**
■ WR's three times a standout **Kimball, Page 100**

12

NFL SCOREBOARD

Rookie Jerome Bidwell runs back 4th yards for a TD as San Diego beats Denver.

CHARGERS..........
BRONCOS..........
RAMS..........
FALCONS..........
SAINTS..........
BUCCANEERS..........
CHARGERS..........
TITANS..........
BROWNS..........
REDSKINS..........
CARDINALS..........
VIKINGS..........

GOTTA HAND IT TO HIM: Patriots quarterback Tom Brady heads to the sideline and coach Bill Belichick after throwing a 60-yard touchdown to David Patten during yesterday's 38-17 victory over the Indianapolis Colts.

NFL Roundup Pages 56, 57

Sports

McGwire bows out
Cards slugger announces his retirement
Page 67

BRUINS try to look afloat after dismal performance in yesterday's Chicago game.

Soccer..........60
Celtics..........65
Auto racing..........61
Colleges..........
Schools..........65
Racing..........54, 53

Forgetta-Bill win

Defense saves day in Patriots' 21-11 victory over Buffalo **Story, Page 78**

NFL SCOREBOARD

Chris Chambers heads up-field in the Dolphins' victory over the Colts. Page 88

DOLPHINS..........
COLTS..........
FALCONS..........
PANTHERS..........
RAMS..........
BEARS..........
49ERS..........
JAGUARS..........
BENGALS..........
STEELERS..........
BRONCOS..........
CHARGERS..........
STEELERS..........
RAVENS..........
VIKINGS..........

SHOW OF HANDS: Patriots fans celebrate along with Antowain Smith after the running back clinched yesterday's 21-11 victory over the Bills with a 42-yard touchdown run in the fourth quarter. Complete coverage, Pages 76-78.

NFL Roundup Pages 60, 61

SUNDAY Sports

PULLOUT SECTION • JANUARY 20, 2002 • BOSTON SUNDAY HERALD

SNOW BOOT
Vinatieri, Pats kick Raiders
Pages B10-B11

13

ON TOP!

Pats push past Miami for lead in AFC East

Pages B2-B12

Prof. Massarotti doesn't hold back on final marks
Grades: Page 70

U.S. men beat Jamaica to earn World Cup bid
Page 68

Pats go south

Take turn for worse in disappointing 30-10 loss to Dolphins Story, Page 78

BAD SIGN: With the large Dolphins logo as a backdrop, Patriots coach Bill Belichick walks the sideline trying to figure out what went wrong during yesterday's 30-10 loss to Miami at Pro Player Stadium. Coverage, Pages 75-79.

MONDAY, OCTOBER 15, 2001 ● BOSTON HERALD, PAGE 112

Back to New York Yankees right back in it with Game 4 victory Page 70

Arizona sparkles Womack delivers D-backs to send D-backs to NLCS Page 68

Lightning strikes

Brady leads late comeback, Patriots beat Chargers in OT Story, Page 108

PUMPED UP: Patriots quarterback Tom Brady celebrates his fourth-quarter touchdown pass to Jermaine Wiggins that turned overtime against the San Diego Chargers yesterday in Foxboro. Adam Vinatieri's 44-yard field goal in the extra period secured a 29-26 victory for the Pats.

Super wrapup Everett, A-B, Bishop Feehan capture titles Pages 80-76

C's take high road Defeat Raptors to close trip with 4-1 mark Page 94

Beyond belief!

Confident Patriots rally past Jets into playoff contention Story, Page 108

ALL TOGETHER NOW: Quarterback Tom Brady (12) is surrounded by his teammates on the final seconds tick away on the Patriots' 17-16 come-from-behind victory over the New York Jets at the Meadowlands yesterday. Complete coverage, Pages 111-96.

Leads team to victory, vents after game Page 86

Giants slugger gets shut out in quest for 70 Page 82

Total dominance

Patriots turn in complete effort in 44-13 pounding of Colts Story, Page 104

RUSH TO JUDGMENT: Antowain Smith (32) is mobbed by his teammates after scoring on a 4-yard touchdown run in the first quarter at Foxboro Stadium yesterday. The Pats didn't stop there as they throttled the Indianapolis Colts, 44-13, for their first victory of the season.

MONDAY, NOVEMBER 26, 2001 ● BOSTON HERALD, PAGE 104

Defense rests Another ranked foe runs over O'Brien, BC Page 68

ALSO INSIDE
BU HOCKEY TEAM fails to sweep Cornell but Matt Turner keys Terriers on the road.
Page 73

Bruins........................90
Celtics........................78
Schools.................67, 66
Lotteries......................58
Racing...................57, 56

Points made

Brady makes move pay off with 4 TDs and win over Saints Story, Page 100

SUPPORT GROUP: Patriots quarterback Tom Brady (right) receives congratulations from Drew Bledsoe after tossing a touchdown pass during yesterday's 34-17 victory over the Saints. Brady threw for four TDs and 268 yards in the win.

WEATHER
JANUARY TRANS: Mostly sunny, breezy and mild. High 48 Lo 53 Page 12

TV listings....................37
Obituaries................24-27
Lotteries.....................64
Classified................59-60
Comparte extra..............2

Find us online:
www.bostonherald.com

BOSTON Herald

MONDAY, JANUARY 28, 2002 ● 50 CENTS

Solemn promise
Cardinal pledges to try settling sex-abuse claims.
Full coverage, Pages 4-6

PATS FANS POUR THEIR HEARTS OUT FOR CHAMPS

BOSTON Herald

SIMPLY SUPER: Thousands of fans line Tremont Street as the Patriots' procession passes by en route to a Government Center rally, for full coverage of the parade and rally honoring the champs, see Pages 14-22, 25, 34 and 98-102.

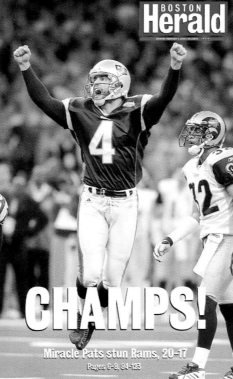

BOSTON Herald

MONDAY, FEBRUARY 4, 2002 ● 50 CENTS

CHAMPS!

Miracle Pats stun Rams, 20-17
Pages 6-8, 84-123

JUBILATION: Patriots kicker Adam Vinatieri jumps for joy after kicking a game-winning field goal on the Superdome last night, lifting the Pats to a 20-17 victory over the Rams in Super Bowl XXXVI.

More Sports

Drew Bledsoe hugs lineman Grant Williams after tossing a TD pass in yesterday's AFC Championship Game. Tom Brady was injured and Bledsoe helped lead the team to a 24-17 victory.

JUST SUPER!

Pats stun Steelers, face Rams in New Orleans Pages 3, 92-120

MONDAY, DECEMBER 10, 2001 ● BOSTON HERALD, PAGE 104

Warming to task Duke needs to act in baseball's winter meetings Page 84

ALSO INSIDE
NEBRASKA GETS national title shot against Miami; BC plays Georgia in Music City bowl.
Page 60

Bruins........................90
Celtics........................78
Colleges.................76-70, 60
Lotteries......................62
Racing...................60, 59

Happy returns

Patriots' special teams shine as Belichick beats old squad Story, Page 100

OFF TO THE RACES: With the help of Lawyer Milloy's block on Cleveland's Dwayne Rudd (57), Patriots punt returner Troy Brown breaks through en route to an 85-yard touchdown in the second quarter of yesterday's 27-16 victory over the Browns at Foxboro Stadium.

MONDAY, JANUARY 28, 2002 ● BOSTON HERALD, PAGE 104

Rams back in Bowl Warner, St. Louis hold off stingy Eagles Page 90

ALSO INSIDE
Bruins........................90
Celtics........................84
Colleges.................82-74
Schools..................70-70
Lotteries......................64
Red Sox......................63
Racing...................62, 61

Bayou-bound!

Pats upset Steelers to earn Super Bowl berth against Rams Story, Page 116

BOSTON Herald

TUESDAY, FEBRUARY 5, 2002 ● 50 CENTS

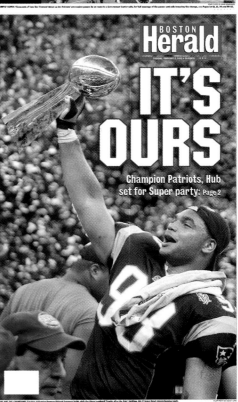

IT'S OURS

Champion Patriots, Hub set for Super party: Page 2

WE ARE THE CHAMPIONS: Patriots defensive lineman Richard Seymour holds aloft the Vince Lombardi Trophy after the Pats' thrilling, 20-17 Super Bowl victory Sunday night.

PATS ROSTER A CONSTUCTION SITE

Michael Felger; Boston Herald

Patriots fans generally regard the 2000 season as a rebuilding year. If only that were the case. Given the decimated roster and bloated salary cap he inherited from the previous regime, Bill Belichick never really got a chance to rebuild last season. The Pats' head coach and chief decision-maker was too busy tearing down and cleaning up.

"You said it, not me," said Belichick. "I certainly wouldn't argue with that. But we did lay down the foundation. We did some things, not nearly as many as I would have liked, but the team learned how to work, how to practice hard. We integrated a lot of young players. It was painful, but now it's better."

In many ways, Belichick and personnel director Scott Pioli were given a pass last year, when the roster was filled with Bobby Grier draft picks and the locker room was making an attitude adjustment after three years under Pete Carroll. Now Belichick has drastically retooled the roster in his image, and only six Grier draft picks remain. If the Pats don't improve on last year's 5-11 season, then Belichick is the one responsible.

So call this the Pats' first true rebuilding year under Belichick and Pioli. Here's how they're doing it.

The salary cap: Putting sentiment aside, Belichick began clearing the dead wood early and hasn't stopped. Ben Coates, Bruce Armstrong, Zefross Moss, Todd Rucci, Max Lane, Chris Slade, Larry Whigham, Henry Thomas and Tony Simmons have all bitten the dust. In each case, their on-field production couldn't justify their price tags.

Meanwhile, because of salary cap implications, some players couldn't be released. But they could be restructured. So Ted Johnson accepted a pay cut and Willie McGinest agreed to a massive restructure.

Lastly, the Pats changed the way they do big contracts. The days of huge signing bonuses and back-loaded deals are over. That's what the Pats did with the likes of Johnson, McGinest and Ty Law—and they're paying for it now. The new deals contain stable base salaries and layered signing bonuses. The Pats determined that Drew Bledsoe, for example, is an $8 million-a-year player, so that's what his cap numbers will hover around every year. He won't count $4 million against the cap one year and $12 million the next.

As a result, the Pats are in the best cap shape they've been in for years. They had the room to sign 22 veteran free agents in the offseason while carving out new deals for Bledsoe and first-round pick Richard Seymour. Next year, they'll be in even better shape.

The draft: Belichick and Pioli say it wasn't a predetermined strategy, but looking back, there was a clear emphasis on the trenches in their first two drafts. Of the seven players still on the roster drafted in Rounds 1-4, four were offensive linemen (Adrian Klemm, Greg Robinson-Randall, Matt Light, Kenyatta Jones) and one was a defensive lineman (Seymour). Meanwhile, the offensive skill positions were largely ignored, with only running back J.R. Redmond figuring to have an impact this season.

SUPER BOWL CHAMPIONS

Depth: Almost immediately after taking over, Belichick and Pioli determined this was their No. 1 priority. So once they got the salary cap in order, they scoured the league for veteran help at nearly every position on the roster. This offseason, they came up with four receivers (Charles Johnson, David Patten, Bert Emanuel and Torrance Small), four linebackers (Larry Izzo, Mike Vrabel, Bryan Cox and Roman Phifer), three defensive backs (Terrell Buckley, Terrance Shaw and Je'Rod Cherry), two offensive linemen (Mike Compton and Joe Panos), two defensive linemen (Anthony Pleasant and Riddick Parker), a tight end (Johnny McWilliams), a running back (Antowain Smith), a fullback (Marc Edwards) and a potential backup quarter-back (Damon Huard).

Not all of the signings panned out (Panos retired and McWilliams was cut), but the vast majority will play a role this year. And they'll do it for cheap dollars. The above group will cost the Pats less than $10 million against the cap in 2001. By comparison, Bledsoe and Law will cost $13.5 million alone.

"We knew there was a number of things we had to improve," said Pioli. "A lot of teams look at free agency and say, 'If we spend a lot of money on this one player, or these three players, that will fill the needs we have.' Well, we felt we had more than three problems."

Third-down offense and defense: For years, the Pats have been a dreadful third-down team on both sides of the ball. So Belichick and Pioli addressed it. This year, look for Buckley, Shaw and Phifer to help in nickel coverage schemes; look for Cox on the pass rush; look for Small over the middle and in traffic; and look for Smith in short-yardage situations.

Toughness and character: The perception that Carroll ran a soft outfit apparently rang true to Belichick. As a result, nearly every player signed or drafted was done with leadership and toughness in mind. Compton, Cox, Izzo, Light and Matt Stevens all fit the mold.

So the Pats are tougher. But does that make them better?

"Yes," said Belichick. 'It's a long season. In this league, where it comes down to just a few plays in so many games, situations where physical and mental toughness determines how you respond to pressure, it's all part of it. Staying power. Resiliency. Those things were not a great area of strength for us last year."

The future: As an organization, the Pats believe big-money free agency is not the way to build a team. But that doesn't mean they've totally taken it out of the game plan.

"I don't know if there's a right or wrong way," said Belichick. "I looked at the situation we were in and tried to make the most of it. We had very little flexibility last year. We had more this year, but still not a lot. I felt that depth was the No. 1 weakness—still do—so that meant getting a lot of guys. Even that meant losing one or two of our guys, like (starting nose tackle) Chad Eaton.

"Next year the situation will be different and maybe we'll take a different approach."

In the meantime, the building continues.

SUPER BOWL CHAMPIONS

CLASSY TILL THE END

CLASSY TILL THE END

CLASSY TILL THE END

CLASSY TILL THE END

Mark Murphy, Boston Herald

BLEDSOE

In the end Drew Bledsoe didn't change. He was there to deliver every bit of advice, every slap on the back.

He loved it when Bill Belichick handed Tom Brady the keys to the car and told him to drive the team downfield with 1:21 left instead of playing it safe.

Bledsoe went up to Brady and excitedly gave his fellow quarterback a boost.

"I told him to sling it," Bledsoe said after the Patriots' 20-17 win over the Rams last night in Super Bowl XXXVI. "That's what legends are made of—a two-minute drive to win the game.

"I was trying and lobbying with the coaches to go ahead and do that," he said. "Let's go and win this now. Right now. It just felt great when (offensive coordinator Charlie Weis) came over and said that's exactly what they were going to do."

Bledsoe's only regret—a heavy, unspoken one —was that he wasn't out there taking those final snaps.

But his own legend is on hold at the moment, and nothing that happened last night was about to change it.

The quarterback, who was in tears after the Pats' 24-17 AFC championship win over Pittsburgh with the realization that it would probably be his last action as a Patriot, was not anxious to look ahead last night.

Like everyone else—and especially that group of nine Patriots who returned to the Superdome for the Super Bowl for the second time in five years last night—he had shed a lot of sweat and grief for last night's supreme reward.

Though Brady was named MVP of the Super Bowl, virtually cementing Bledsoe's trade to another team, the mentor was not in a rush to meet his favorite tarot card reader at Jackson Square last night.

"Right now I'm just going to enjoy this feeling," Bledsoe said. "As far as the future goes, I don't know.

SUPER BOWL CHAMPIONS

"I'm excited for the future, I can't wait to play again, and we'll see what happens from here," he said.

And so Bledsoe closed out the same way he has ever since it became apparent Brady would lead this team: He said all the right things.

He walked out with the rest of the team during introductions and savored the fact they were introduced as a group, not individually.

"We've done it that way all year—in total team style," he said. "Everyone did their part. Everyone contributed."

Including one very proud quarterback.

THINGS LOOK BAD AGAIN
PATS TAKE HEAVY FALL VS. BENGALS

Michael Felger; Boston Herald

A bad offensive line. A porous, un-clutch defense. A late rally that came up short. Drew Bledsoe on the ground, needing to be helped off the field after another futile, fourth-quarter heave.

Sound familiar?

Like a recurring bad dream, the horrors of the Patriots' anemic 2000 season repeated themselves at Paul Brown Stadium yesterday. The lowly Bengals were supposed to offer the Pats a prime opportunity to begin 2001 on a winning note. Instead, it was just more of the same as the Pats dropped the opener, 23-17.

Tell us if you've heard these words before. "We had our chances," said coach Bill Belichick. "I felt we had them on the ropes. We just couldn't make enough plays when we needed them."

As was so often the case last year, this game featured plenty to dissect and debate. One play in particular seemed to stick out. With the Pats down by six and facing a fourth-and-2 at the Bengals' 41-yard line, Bledsoe inexplicably called his own number on a quarterback sneak. Bledsoe, a notoriously poor sneak quarterback, was close, but the Pats lost the measurement by a razor-thin margin.

Belichick was clearly flustered, and when Bledsoe got off the field, words were exchanged. Belichick said the sneak was a "combination" between Bledsoe's discretion and the play called from the sideline. Center Damien Woody and Bledsoe said it was the quarterback's call.

"You see a certain defense and you audible to it," said Woody. "I thought we had it, but it turned out differently."

Added Bledsoe: "I thought I could pick up the yard or the yard and a half, whatever it was."

The replacement officials were called on to make several close calls, and video replay was frequently in use. The Pats got the benefit of some of the calls (a Jermaine Wiggins fourth-quarter score) and were on the short end of others (an apparent Bert Emanuel catch that was overturned on the game's final possession).

But close plays or not, the Pats didn't deserve to win with the way they played in the third quarter. That's when Cincinnati put 13 points on the board while the Pats could manage only 9 yards of offense and no first downs.

In fairness, with their No. 1 draft pick, nose tackle Richard Seymour (leg), and middle linebacker Ted Johnson (hip) both out of action, the Pats were very soft up the middle. Corey Dillon took advantage with 104 yards and a touchdown on 24 carries. But if the run defense had a legitimate excuse, the pass defense didn't. The Pats once again made a bad quarterback look like a great one as Jon Kitna completed 18-of-27 passes for 204 yards and a touchdown.

And the offensive line? Yikes. Bledsoe was sacked four times and hit nearly twice as often while back Antowain Smith could manage just 33 yards on 11 carries.

There were some good signs for the Patriots, who converted both of their red zone opportunities while showing some rhythm on offense. Bledsoe (22-of-38, 241 yards, two touchdowns) was at times very effective. But when Kitna hit a wide open Tim McGee over the middle to make it 23-10 late in the third quarter, the Pats once again found themselves with too big a hill to climb.

"I'm disappointed in myself," said linebacker Bryan Cox, hopefully setting a tone of responsibility. "I had too many plays I wish I could have had back. You can't be afraid to say it: 'I can do more.' "

Unless they want another year like 2000, the Pats had BETTER do more.

SUPER BOWL CHAMPIONS

"We had our chances. I felt we had them on the ropes. We just couldn't make enough plays when we needed them."

PATRIOTS COACH BILL BELICHICK

	1st	2nd	3rd	4th	Final
New England	0	10	0	7	17
Cincinnati	0	10	13	0	23

SCORING SUMMARY

QTR	TEAM	PLAY		TIME
2nd	**PATRIOTS** TD	Brown 14-yd. pass from Bledsoe (Vinatieri kick)	....	14:55
2nd	**BENGALS** FG	Rackers 36-yd.	....	11:22
2nd	**PATRIOTS** FG	Vinatieri 39-yd.	....	6:04
2nd	**BENGALS** TD	Dillon 5-yd. run (Rackers kick)	....	2:16
3rd	**BENGALS** FG	Rackers 47-yd.	....	12:05
3rd	**BENGALS** FG	Rackers 33-yd.	....	6:01
3rd	**BENGALS** TD	McGee 25-yd. pass from Kitna (Rackers kick)	....	0:06
4th	**PATRIOTS** TD	Wiggins 8-yd. pass from Bledsoe (Vinatieri kick)	....	5:29

OFFENSE

PATRIOTS

PASSING	ATT	COMP	YDS	INT	TD
Bledsoe	38	22	241	0	2

RECEIVING	ATT	YDS	TD
Brown	7	106	1
Patten	3	47	0
Emanuel	4	25	0
Redmond	3	24	0
Wiggins	3	24	1
Pass	1	11	0
Johnson	1	4	0

RUSHING	ATT	YDS	TD
Smith	11	33	0
Edwards	4	13	0
Redmond	3	12	0
Bledsoe	3	10	0

BENGALS

PASSING	ATT	COMP	YDS	INT	TD
Kitna	27	18	204	0	1

RECEIVING	ATT	YDS	TD
Scott	5	104	0
Warrick	7	38	0
Dillon	4	32	0
McGee	1	25	0
Dugans	1	5	0

RUSHING	ATT	YDS	TD
Dillon	20	83	0
Bennett	6	3	0
Warrick	1	1	0
Kitna	2	-3	0

BLEDSOE, PATRIOTS KO'D
QB HEADS TO HOSPITAL AFTER LOSS TO JETS

Michael Felger; Boston Herald

An inspired and dramatic pregame ceremony at Foxboro Stadium yesterday gave way to an afternoon of football that was anything but. The result was another loss for the Patriots.

The Pats are now 0-2 after a 10-3 defeat to the Jets, but the big news surrounds quarterback Drew Bledsoe. After taking a hard hit by Jets linebacker Mo Lewis late in the fourth quarter, Bledsoe was held out by coach Bill Belichick for the final series in favor of second-year quarterback Tom Brady.

It was learned last night that Bledsoe was taken to Mass. General Hospital to have his ribs examined. Test results were not known.

Belichick said he lifted Bledsoe based on how the quarterback looked and played on the series following the Lewis hit. The coach was justifiably concerned. After the game, Bledsoe was wheeled out on a stretcher and into an awaiting ambulance.

Bledsoe suffered the injury while trying to run for a first down along the sideline. That's where he ran into Lewis. Bledsoe returned for the next possession, which featured two running plays and a short pass. From that, Belichick deduced that Bledsoe was done.

"He said he was OK and I thought he was OK, but he probably wasn't," said Belichick. "I shouldn't have put him back out there. We put Brady in because we didn't feel (Bledsoe) was ready to go."

Teammates were surprised to see the franchise quarterback on the sideline with the game hanging in the balance. They were even more surprised to see him standing up after the hit he took from Lewis.

"He got hit as hard as I think I've seen anyone get hit," said Brady, who drove the Pats 46 yards on five completions but came up short on two desperation throws into the end zone as time expired.

"That hit Drew took was unbelievable," said another teammate. "You would think they would keep him in there just for taking that hit and coming back."

As for the game, it came down to the Pats' offense being unable to make plays. The turnovers told the story, as the Pats had four—all on the Jets' side of the field—while New York had none.

Bledsoe (two interceptions) will surely get much of the blame, but he's far from the only culprit. The Pats had trouble handling the ball, and shotgun snapper Mike Compton, receiver Bert Emanuel and fullback Marc Edwards were all guilty. Edwards, in particular, hurt the Pats with two fumbles. The first came on the Jets' 7-yard line after Bledsoe had driven the Pats down the field on the opening drive of the third quarter.

Edwards said it was the low-point of his five-year career.

"Definitely," said Edwards, who had a fine day otherwise with 31 rushing yards and six receptions (22 yards), both team highs. "I was brought in here to make plays and be one of the guys to be counted on. But that wasn't the case today."

Ex-Patriot Curtis Martin was typically effective with 106 yards and a touchdown on 24

SUPER BOWL CHAMPIONS

carries. The Pats defense was decent, but they gave up two long scoring drives that spelled defeat. The decisive one started after the first Edwards fumble, lasted 12 plays and ended on Martin's 8-yard touchdown run.

"It was a real tough loss," said a clearly ruffled Belichick. "It's just too bad. I felt like the team really deserved better."

In the locker room, players did their best to keep a positive outlook. But the reality of the situation was also crystal clear.

Said safety Lawyer Milloy: "0-2 is 0-2. That's unacceptable—0-2 sucks."

"It was a real tough loss. It's just too bad. I felt like the team really deserved better."

PATRIOTS COACH BILL BELICHICK

SUPER BOWL CHAMPIONS

	1st	2nd	3rd	4th	Final
NY Jets	0	3	7	0	10
New England	3	0	0	0	3

SCORING SUMMARY

QTR	TEAM	PLAY		TIME
1st	**PATRIOTS**	FG	Vinatieri 24-yd.	0:52
2nd	**JETS**	FG	Hall 26-yd.	0:00
3rd	**JETS**	TD	Martin 8-yd. run (Hall kick)	2:29

OFFENSE

PATRIOTS

PASSING	ATT	COMP	YDS	INT	TD
Bledsoe	28	18	159	2	0
Brady	10	5	46	0	0

RECEIVING	ATT	YDS	TD
Brown	5	82	0
Patten	5	53	0
Edwards	6	22	0
Johnson	2	18	0
Redmond	2	16	0
Rutledge	2	10	0
Pass	1	4	0

RUSHING	ATT	YDS	TD
Edwards	6	31	0
Redmond	4	20	0
Smith	10	20	0
Faulk	3	19	0
Brady	1	9	0
Bledsoe	2	8	0

JETS

PASSING	ATT	COMP	YDS	INT	TD
Testaverde	28	16	137	0	0

RECEIVING	ATT	YDS	TD
Chrebet	5	53	0
Becht	2	24	0
Coles	3	24	0
Swayne	1	16	0
Anderson	2	10	0
Martin	3	10	0

RUSHING	ATT	YDS	TD
Martin	24	106	1
Anderson	3	5	0

SUPER BOWL CHAMPIONS

EMOTIONAL DAY
EMOTIONAL DAY
EMOTIONAL DAY
EMOTIONAL DAY
FOR ANDRUZZI FAMILY

Ed Gray, Boston Herald

Three men proudly wearing No.63 Patriots game jerseys made their way to the elevator at Foxboro Stadium yesterday, clearly lacking the enthusiasm customarily shown by fans who are about to take in a Patriots game from the luxury boxes.

An NFL game couldn't take the visiting New York firemen's minds off the devastation at Ground Zero of the World Trade Center that they left behind to attend yesterday's Patriots-Jets game.

"In some sense, I feel like I shouldn't be here," said Jimmy Andruzzi, one of Patriots guard Joe Andruzzi's three brothers who have been involved in rescue operations at the WTC. "I feel I should be back there doing something. But the effort's so dismal that I figured that I might as well take a day off and come up here."

Jimmy, Marc and Billy Andruzzi, along with their father Bill, a retired New York City police officer, were the Patriots' honorary captains for the game's opening coin toss.

The search and rescue mission at Ground Zero has been an overwhelming and discouraging process for the Andruzzis.

"It's futile," said Billy, who was among nine family members in a group of 20 that came to Foxboro Stadium. "We just keep finding more bodies and parts."

Billy, who has spent as much as 16 hours a day at the WTC, said the destruction is greater than anyone outside the rescue mission could imagine.

"TV doesn't do it justice. Being there is the only way you can understand how bad it is," he said. "No one can know how devastating it's been for New York City, the police and firemen and the victims."

Although the brave trio may have had mixed feelings about leaving such devastation behind yesterday, Bill Andruzzi was happy to accompany his sons to Foxboro.

"They really need this at this point," said the Andruzzi family's patriarch. "Not to discount any other firemen and policemen and other service people who risked their lives, but they went through a

SUPER BOWL CHAMPIONS

traumatic experience. What Boston, Massachusetts and Foxboro and Mr. (Patriots owner Bob) Kraft have done for them is fantastic."

Joe was overcome when he saw his brothers yesterday.

"No words were said. We just hugged and I cried," he said.

The Patriots guard was also touched by the crowd's reaction to his brothers and father.

"It was a great honor for them being recognized as heroes," he said.

DEFENSE SETS TONE IN
44-13 SHOCKER

Michael Felger; Boston Herald

In a sign of unity, the Patriots defense eschewed the traditional pregame introduction yesterday. Instead of having each player introduced individually, the entire 11-man unit came onto the field as one, arms waving and fists pumping.

It turned out to be a prophetic gesture, because the Patriots' stunning 44-13 upset win over the Indianapolis Colts at Foxboro Stadium was one thing above all others: A total team victory.

"We're not a bad football team," said linebacker Bryan Cox, who set the verbal tone earlier in the week and the physical tone on the first series yesterday. "We suffer a little from confidence problems because of what's gone on here the past few years. But we did what I thought we could do."

Historically, the Colts have struggled against Bill Belichick defenses and at Foxboro Stadium. That was once again the case as the Colts couldn't handle the windy weather or the hostile environment. Peyton Manning and Edgerrin James remain winless in Foxboro, where the Colts have now lost eight of their last nine.

"It was a great win," said Belichick, whose team takes a 1-2 record into Miami next weekend. "I felt we really needed it. The players really deserved it."

Belichick said it was a "complementary" game in which the Pats got big performances in all three phases of the game. Fans are sure to hear the names Tom Brady, Antowain Smith and Otis Smith all week, but everyone played a part.

The defense was huge, with Cox' thundering hit on Jerome Pathon the first of many big plays. What followed was a stout run defense and huge interceptions from the secondary. Cox (11 tackles) and Bobby Hamilton (four tackles, sack) were the forces up front, while Otis Smith (a 78-yard interception return for a TD) and Ty Law (a 23-yard interception return for a TD) got the glory.

Safety Lawyer Milloy said the Pats realized earlier in the week that they could out-tough the Colts. That toughness, and a "Cover-2" scheme, neutralized Manning (196 yards, three interceptions), James (55 yards on 17 carries) and Marvin Harrison (three catches).

"Watching the film, the one edge we felt we had was being physical," Milloy said. "The tempo was set when Bryan hit (Pathon) over the middle. I don't know how many balls they dropped after that, but it was definitely a factor."

The offense was almost as impressive, especially the running game, which amassed a whopping 177 yards. Anotwain Smith finished with 94 yards and two touchdowns.

Of course, there is sure to be a new quarterback controversy surrounding Brady, the second-year pro who was steady and poised in completing 13-of-23 passes for 168 yards and no touchdowns or interceptions. Brady wasn't asked to do too much, but he still showed more than Drew Bledsoe did over the first two weeks.

At the very least, the Pats have a young leader. If Cox' attitude speaks for the defense, then Brady's confidence bodes well on offense.

"It just seemed like our day," Brady said. "I expected to go out there and do well. I've been preparing for this all along. It's not like they pulled me off the street and said, 'You're starting.'"

The Pats hope the performance is the sign of things to come.

"We believe we have a good team," Milloy said. "It's time to step up and start dictating the play."

Added Cox, who on Wednesday said that the Colts could be beat: "Everyone is happy. Everyone is rejuvenated. But we haven't done anything yet. We have to continue to press. We didn't win the Super Bowl today. We've got a game next week."

SUPER BOWL CHAMPIONS

“ **It was a great win. I felt we really needed it. The players really deserved it.** ”

PATRIOTS COACH BILL BELICHICK

	1st	2nd	3rd	4th	Final
Indianapolis	0	0	7	6	13
New England	7	13	3	21	44

SCORING SUMMARY

Qtr	Team	Play	Time
1st	**PATRIOTS**	TD A. Smith 4-yd. run (Vinatieri kick)	4:23
2nd	**PATRIOTS**	FG Vinatieri 47-yd.	5:50
2nd	**PATRIOTS**	TD O. Smith 78-yd. interception return (Vinatieri kick)	1:42
2nd	**PATRIOTS**	FG Vinatieri 48-yd.	0:00
3rd	**PATRIOTS**	FG Vinatieri 35-yd.	9:37
3rd	**COLTS**	TD Manning 10-yd. run (Vanderjagt kick)	0:53
4th	**PATRIOTS**	TD Faulk 8-yd. run (Vinatieri kick)	13:24
4th	**PATRIOTS**	TD Law 23-yd. interception return (Vinatieri kick)	12:24
4th	**COLTS**	TD Pollard 17-yd. pass from Manning (2-pt. conv. failed)	8:51
4th	**PATRIOTS**	TD A. Smith 2-yd. run (Vinatieri kick)	3:39

OFFENSE

PATRIOTS

PASSING	ATT	COMP	YDS	INT	TD
Brady	23	13	168	0	0

RECEIVING	ATT	YDS	TD
Smith	3	58	0
Faulk	2	38	0
Brown	3	21	0
Small	2	20	0
Patten	1	17	0
Wiggins	1	11	0
Johnson	1	3	0

RUSHING	ATT	YDS	TD
Smith	22	94	2
Faulk	9	48	1
Brown	2	11	0
Edwards	4	11	0
Patten	1	11	0
Brady	1	2	0

COLTS

PASSING	ATT	COMP	YDS	INT	TD
Manning	34	20	196	3	1
Rypien	9	5	57	0	0

RECEIVING	ATT	YDS	TD
Pollard	4	63	1
Pathon	5	57	0
Harrison	3	49	0
James	6	38	0
Wilkins	3	15	0
Insley	2	12	0
Dilger	1	11	0
Rhodes	1	8	0

RUSHING	ATT	YDS	TD
James	17	55	0
Rhodes	4	21	0
Manning	2	14	1
Pathon	1	-8	0

SUPER BOWL CHAMPIONS

A BAD DAY ALL AROUND
PATS SUFFER LOSS IN ROUT BY FISH

Michael Felger; Boston Herald

If last week's upset victory over Indianapolis was a total team effort by the Patriots, then so was yesterday's showing at Pro Player Stadium. The results, of course, were far different—and when passing out blame for the 30-10 loss to the Dolphins, no one should be spared.

The Patriots were alarmingly weak on defense, anemic on offense and mistake-prone on special teams. They got beat in the trenches and in the open field. Young Tom Brady looked like the inexperienced second-year quarterback that he is, while old Bryan Cox couldn't provide the emotional spark.

It all spelled a lopsided defeat to a superior team on a sweltering day in the Miami heat. Afterward, the question was asked over and over: How could a Pats team that looked so good against the Colts be so bad just seven days later?

"Last week was last week and this week is this week—that's the explanation," said Cox (three tackles). "They were able to enforce their will on us. It was a total butt-kicking. No excuses."

The "butt-kicking" theme was repeated early and often in the locker room—and for good reason. The Pats made Dolphins running back Lamar Smith (144 yards) look like Walter Payton and quarterback Jay Fiedler (87 passing yards, 37 rushing yards) look like Doug Flutie. This just a week after the Pats stuffed two superior players in Edgerrin James and Peyton Manning.

"We can't be one-hit wonders," said Pats safety Lawyer Milloy. "We can't be collectively good as a team one game and then come out and do what we did today."

The Pats are now 1-3 on the year and risk fading into irrelevance if they come out on the short end of next week's meeting against Flutie and the San Diego Chargers.

"We need to refocus and regenerate our efforts to be a more efficient football team," said coach Bill Belichick. "We can't be donors, we have to make opponents work for it. We're too generous. That's where it starts."

It also starts in practice during the week, a place where Brady said the Pats were sorely lacking last week. The second-year pro promised it would be better in the future.

"We just have to fight our way out of this and there's nobody who is going to help us," he said. "Everyone is going to tell us how bad we are now—but we are the only ones who can affect how we play."

Brady did not play well yesterday, completing just 12-of-24 passes for 86 yards. Brady's fumble deep in Pats territory in the third quarter (which both he and center Damien Woody took the blame for) resulted in a 1-yard touchdown return for Jason Taylor and put the game out of reach at 27-10. Belichick said he never considered lifting Brady for veteran backup Damon Huard.

Afterward, Brady met with Huard and offensive coordinator Charlie Weis and then spent a few moments with Milloy. It was clear that seeds were being planted for next week.

SUPER BOWL CHAMPIONS

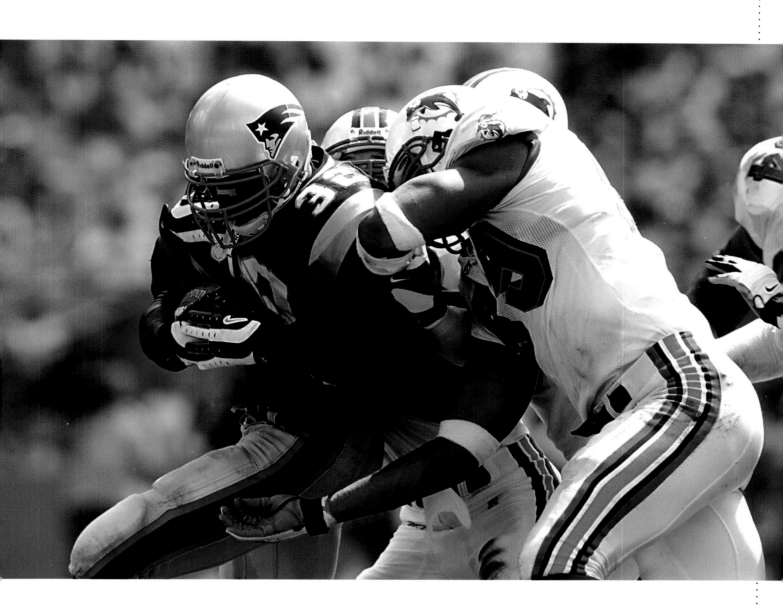

"We're going to rally around him," said Milloy of Brady. "He's in that position. He's still a leader in my eye."

The game, which kicked off right as President Bush was addressing the nation over air strikes in Afghanistan, started well enough for the Pats as an interception by Mike Vrabel deep in Dolphins territory set up a 9-yard touchdown run by Antowain Smith (47 yards on 14 carries).

But from there it was all Dolphins, with the key sequence coming just before the half. With the game tied at 10, Miami was apparently playing for a field goal before Fiedler sent a 14-yard fade pass into the end zone for tight end Jed Weaver, who beat Tedy Bruschi to haul in the ball for the score.

The spread was seven points at that junction, but it could have been 1,000. This was not the Patriots' day.

SUPER BOWL CHAMPIONS

"**We're going to rally around [Brady]. He's still a leader in my eyes.**"

PATRIOTS SAFETY LAWYER MILLOY

	1st	2nd	3rd	4th	Final
New England	7	3	0	0	10
Miami	7	10	10	3	30

SCORING SUMMARY

QTR	TEAM	PLAY		TIME
1st	**PATRIOTS**	TD	A. Smith 9-yd. run (Vinatieri kick)	12:03
1st	**DOLPHINS**	TD	L. Smith 7-yd. run (Mare kick)	3:39
2nd	**DOLPHINS**	FG	Mare 19-yd.	14:21
2nd	**PATRIOTS**	FG	Vinatieri 37-yd.	6:42
2nd	**DOLPHINS**	TD	Weaver 14-yd. pass from Fiedler (Mare kick)	0:07
3rd	**DOLPHINS**	FG	Mare 34-yd.	7:58
3rd	**DOLPHINS**	TD	Taylor 1-yd. fumble return (Mare kick)	0:00
4th	**DOLPHINS**	FG	Mare 27-yd.	2:08

OFFENSE

PATRIOTS

PASSING	ATT	COMP	YDS	INT	TD
Brady	24	12	86	0	0

RECEIVING	ATT	YDS	TD
Brown	5	47	0
Faulk	2	15	0
Patten	1	10	0
Small	2	9	0
Edwards	1	4	0
Smith	1	1	0

RUSHING	ATT	YDS	TD
Smith	14	47	1
Edwards	3	14	0
Faulk	4	10	0
Brady	2	9	0

DOLPHINS

PASSING	ATT	COMP	YDS	INT	TD
Fiedler	21	11	87	1	1

RECEIVING	ATT	YDS	TD
Smith	3	23	0
Gadsden	2	21	0
McKinght	2	17	0
Weaver	1	14	1
Ward	1	10	0
Ogden	1	3	0
Minor	1	-1	0

RUSHING	ATT	YDS	TD
Smith	29	144	1
Fiedler	7	37	0
Minor	7	25	0
McKinght	1	3	0

SUPER BOWL CHAMPIONS

BRADY POWERS OVERTIME WIN

Michael Felger; Boston Herald

Tom Brady stood in a near-empty Patriots locker room late yesterday afternoon while Terry Glenn spoke to the assembled media in an adjacent room and Bill Belichick headed down the hall to offer a few choice words to the referees. After an emotional, draining day, Brady's face was fresh and his voice was strong.

"You're 1-3, you're down 10 points and your season is basically make-or-break," the 24-year-old quarterback said following the Pats' heart-stopping, come-from-behind, 29-26 overtime win over San Diego. "What happened today just shows that the guys in here want to fight. It shows that when you're willing to put it all on the line, good things happen."

Brady and the Pats put it all on the line yesterday, and the result was a 44-yard Adam Vinatieri field goal with four minutes gone in the extra session—and the biggest win of the Belichick era. Earlier in the week, the Pats coach buried the game ball from last week's Miami loss in the practice fields behind Foxboro Stadium. Today, his 2-3 Pats are alive to see another day.

Overcoming horrendous special teams, typically shoddy third-down defense and some highly questionable officiating, Brady and the Pats took down Doug Flutie and the Chargers. The schedule takes a decided turn for the worse with games at Indianapolis and Denver the next two weeks, but at least the Pats are in the picture.

"It was a terrific win for this football team," said Belichick. "The players showed a lot of courage."

Added safety Lawyer Milloy: "It showed we have some heart."

This was a game that was decided over the final 20 minutes of action. The Pats' special teams were simply awful all day ("The worst in a year and a half," said Belichick), and punter Lee Johnson's fumble at the Pats' 6-yard line was the icing on the cake. Derrick Harris' recovery and touchdown gave the Chargers a 26-16 lead with 8:48 left in regulation.

Johnson held on to the ball to avoid the rush, but he fumbled as he tried to carry the ball with one hand above his right shoulder. It was a bad-looking play with a bad result. "I tried to spin and make a play," said Johnson. "But I couldn't get away."

That sent many fans to the exits, but Brady remained strong. Showing remarkable poise and leadership, Brady completed 10-of-16 passes for 101 yards over the final two drives. The tying score came on a 3-yard toss to tight end Jermaine Wiggins with 40 seconds left in regulation.

After Chargers placekicker Wade Richey came up short on a 59-yard field goal attempt as regulation time expired, Brady picked up a key interior blitz in overtime, which led to a 37-yard interference penalty on receiver David Patten. A few plays later, Vinatieri knocked home the winner.

Brady finished with some eye-popping numbers (33-of-54 for 364 yards, two touchdowns, no interceptions), but he was only one of many sidelights to the game. There was the return of Glenn (seven catches for 110 yards and a touchdown), the redemption of Vinatieri (he earlier missed an extra point and a 44-yard field goal) and the re-emergence of Wiggins, who had gone two

full games without having a pass thrown his way. On Friday, Wiggins had to listen as Belichick criticized the play of his tight ends this year.

"Of course you take that to heart," Wiggins said of Belichick's criticism. "You just continue to work hard and when they call your number you hope you make the play."

Then there was Glenn, who put aside all the "bad blood" to have a scintillating, athletic performance.

"The biggest lift for us was Terry Glenn being back in the mix," cornerback Ty Law said emphatically. "You guys (the media) need to leave him alone. That should quiet you up now."

Meanwhile, the team will try to continue on the road back to respectability.

"It would have been a long season had we lost," said defensive lineman Bobby Hamilton. "We needed this game. It just shows you that if we continue to believe in ourselves, we can do a lot of things."

> "We needed this game. It just shows you that if we continue to believe in ourselves, we can do a lot of things."
>
> PATRIOTS LINEMAN
> BOBBY HAMILTON

SUPER BOWL CHAMPIONS

	1st	2nd	3rd	4th	OT	Final
San Diego	3	3	7	13	0	26
New England	3	6	7	10	3	29

SCORING SUMMARY

Qtr	Team	Play	Time
1st	**PATRIOTS**	FG Vinatieri 26-yd.	9:56
1st	**CHARGERS**	FG Richey 21-yd.	0:00
2nd	**PATRIOTS**	TD Glenn 21-yd. pass from Brady (PAT failed)	3:55
2nd	**CHARGERS**	FG Richey 27-yd.	0:29
3rd	**CHARGERS**	TD Tomlinson 1-yd. run (Richey kick)	9:43
3rd	**PATRIOTS**	TD A. Smith 1-yd. run (Vinatieri kick)	4:20
4th	**CHARGERS**	TD Heiden 3-yd. pass from Flutie (2-pt. conv. failed)	10:00
4th	**CHARGERS**	TD Harris 6-yd. fumble return (Richey kick)	8:48
4th	**PATRIOTS**	FG Vinatieri 23-yd.	3:31
4th	**PATRIOTS**	TD Wiggins 3-yd. pass from Brady (Vinatieri kick)	0:36
OT	**PATRIOTS**	FG Vinatieri 44-yd.	10:55

OFFENSE

PATRIOTS

PASSING	ATT	COMP	YDS	INT	TD
Brady	54	33	364	0	2

RECEIVING	ATT	YDS	TD
Brown	11	117	0
Glenn	7	110	1
Patten	7	73	0
Faulk	2	21	0
Edwards	1	15	0
Pass	1	9	0
Smith	2	9	0
Cox	1	7	0
Wiggins	1	3	1

RUSHING	ATT	YDS	TD
Smith	15	36	1
Pass	1	7	0
Edwards	4	5	0
Brady	1	0	0
Faulk	2	0	0
Johnson	1	-19	0

CHARGERS

PASSING	ATT	COMP	YDS	INT	TD
Flutie	32	20	270	0	1

RECEIVING	ATT	YDS	TD
Conway	4	117	0
Dwight	3	54	0
Graham	4	43	0
Jones	2	15	0
Fletcher	2	14	0
Tomlinson	3	13	0
Jones	1	11	0
Heiden	1	3	1

RUSHING	ATT	YDS	TD
Tomlinson	24	74	1
Fletcher	1	8	0
McCrary	1	2	0
Flutie	2	1	0

SUPER BOWL CHAMPIONS

PATRIOTS STRIKE AGAIN
BIG PLAY CRUSHES COLTS 38-17

Michael Felger; Boston Herald

The Patriots' two biggest names on offense were on the sidelines in street clothes, and the unit could not have been more lethal. The special teams were just seven days removed from their worst performance in memory, and they hardly could have been more effective. The defense was tested all day, and it couldn't have held any better.

Is it time to start believing yet?

Maybe it is, maybe it isn't. For now, just know that the Patriots have rarely looked better than they did yesterday. There's no other way to say it: The Pats demolished the Indianapolis Colts. The 38-17 final evened their record at 3-3, and fans now have reason to believe that a trip to the playoffs may not be out of the question.

"Big. A huge win," center Damien Woody said. "What we did (yesterday) is what good teams do."

Added coach Bill Belichick, whose offense was without stars Drew Bledsoe (chest) and Terry Glenn (hamstring): "I'm proud of the players and coaches. It was a great game plan, and the players came ready to play."

Did they ever. There were so many big plays, so many impressive numbers, that it's hard to know where to begin.

How about with receiver David Patten, who became the first NFL player since Walter Payton in 1979 to run, catch and throw for a touchdown in the same game?

How about with emerging star Tom Brady, who threw three touchdown passes and continues to play with such poise that a quarterback controversy is all but assured when Bledsoe returns?

How about with a coaching staff that had all the tricks on offense and all the answers on defense?

"Everybody made plays," Brady said. "Guys really came to play, and it showed. It's not often you draw plays up and have them work the way they did for us. It was just our day."

No kidding. The Pats' first 21 points came on one-play drives lasting a total of 30 seconds, and Patten played a part in all three. He ran a 29-yard reverse in for a score, caught a 91-yard bomb from Brady (the longest play from scrimmage in Patriots history) and then threw a 60-yard scoring toss to Troy Brown.

That last play will have fans buzzing for days. Belichick said the play originally called for Brown to throw it to Patten, but once coaches saw Patten heave the ball at practice last week, they decided to switch the roles.

"I was lobbying for it," Patten said. "I said to Troy, 'I don't care what they do. I'm going to throw the ball up, just don't let them intercept it.'"

Brady said he was surprised offensive coordinator Charlie Weis called for the trickery. Brady then relayed the call in the huddle.

SUPER BOWL CHAMPIONS

"I said, 'Well, guys, Charlie has gone a little crazy,'" Brady said.

The Pats' special teams played a huge role, as Brandon Mitchell and Tebucky Jones each blocked a field goal attempt. Mitchell's block led to a 35-yard return by Leonard Myers and set up Patten's reverse.

"Big plays, big plays," Belichick said. "The first one was a 10-point swing. That's what special teams can do for you."

Defensively, it was a typical Belichick vs. Peyton Manning affair. The Colts were able to drive the ball virtually at will, but when it came time to put it in the end zone, they struggled. As a result, the Colts led in time of possession (33:25 to 26:35), first downs (28-19) and total net yards (484-385), but were way behind on the scoreboard.

Can you say "bend but don't break?"

"That's exactly what happened," linebacker

Ted Johnson said. "It's not always pretty, it's not always the way you want it to be. But you have to make the crucial plays at the crucial times."

Meanwhile, the frustrated Colts had to listen as the boos rained down from the RCA Dome rafters. Those sitting at the far end of the press box also were treated to a stream of obscenities from Colts general manager Bill Polian.

"Come off the (expletive) block!" Polian screamed at one point.

"Call a (expletive) time out! What are these (expletive) coaches thinking out there?" he shouted at another.

No wonder Polian was upset. A look at today's AFC East standings shows the Patriots tied for second place with the Jets, a half-game behind the Dolphins and a half-game ahead of the Colts.

Finally, the Pats are back in the mix.

Everybody made plays. Guys really came to play, and it showed. It's not often you draw plays up and have them work the way they did for us. It was just our day.

QUARTERBACK TOM BRADY

	1st	2nd	3rd	4th	Final
New England	7	21	3	7	38
Indianapolis	3	3	11	0	17

SCORING SUMMARY

QTR	TEAM	PLAY		TIME
1st	**PATRIOTS**	TD	Patten 29-yd. run (Vinatieri kick)	10:35
1st	**COLTS**	FG	Vanderjagt 42-yd.	5:44
2nd	**PATRIOTS**	TD	Patten 91-yd. pass from Brady (Vinatieri kick)	8:56
2nd	**PATRIOTS**	TD	Brown 60-yd.pass from Patten (Vinatieri kick)	7:11
2nd	**PATRIOTS**	TD	Wiggins 2-yd. pass from Brady (Vinatieri kick)	1:17
2nd	**COLTS**	FG	Vanderjagt 42-yd.	0:11
3rd	**COLTS**	TD	Harrison 2-yd. pass from Manning (2-pt. conv. succeeds)	8:20
3rd	**PATRIOTS**	FG	Vinatieri 43-yd.	4:34
3rd	**COLTS**	FG	Vanderjagt 42-yd.	1:31
4th	**PATRIOTS**	TD	Patten 6-yd. pass from Brady (Vinatieri kick)	14:02

OFFENSE

PATRIOTS

PASSING	ATT	COMP	YDS	INT	TD
Brady	20	16	202	0	3
Patten	1	1	60	0	1

RECEIVING	ATT	YDS	TD
Brown	8	120	1
Patten	4	117	2
Edwards	2	16	0
Johnson	2	7	0
Wiggins	1	2	1

RUSHING	ATT	YDS	TD
Smith	21	71	0
Patten	1	29	1
Edwards	3	14	0
Brown	1	9	0
Faulk	1	2	0
Redmond	1	0	0
Brady	2	-2	0

COLTS

PASSING	ATT	COMP	YDS	INT	TD
Manning	34	22	335	0	1

RECEIVING	ATT	YDS	TD
Harrison	8	157	1
Pollard	3	61	0
James	4	34	0
Wayne	3	33	0
Dilger	2	32	0
Insley	1	13	0
McKinney	1	5	0

RUSHING	ATT	YDS	TD
James	30	143	0
Rhodes	2	35	0
Manning	2	1	0

ALL THE RIGHT MOVES

ALL THE RIGHT MOVES

ALL THE RIGHT MOVES

ALL THE RIGHT MOVES

BELICHICK PLAY-CALLING PAYS OFF

George Kimball; Boston Herald

Sometime between the time Adam Vinatieri's kick sailed between the uprights and the moment he first held the Vince Lombardi Trophy in his hands, it probably occurred to Bill Belichick that there was a previously unsuspected benefit to winning football's biggest game on the final tick of the clock.

No Gatorade bath.

St. Louis coach Mike Martz was supposed to be the free-wheeling gambler and Belichick the conservative tactician, but when the Patriots got the ball back with a minute and a half to play in Super Bowl XXXVI, Belichick didn't think twice about going for the win right away.

Even though the Patriots had exhausted their supply of timeouts, the Rams had as well, and Belichick sent Tom Brady out to run the two-minute offense when many coaches might have told him to take a knee and take their chances in sudden death rather than do anything that might risk putting the ball back in Kurt Warner's hands.

"We would have done that had the drive not gone well," Belichick said afterward. "We were going to go into our two-minute offense and give it a couple of shots. If we got the ball up the field, we'd stay with it, but if we had gotten sacked or had a negative play in there, we certainly weren't going to give the ball back to the Rams. They were out of timeouts, so we felt we could run a couple of plays and, at the worst, run out the clock if we didn't pick up any yardage on the early part of the drive."

Once Brady hit Troy Brown on the 23-yard pass that got the Patriots to the 36, the die was cast.

"We'd have been looking at, what, 58 yards (53, actually)? At least we'd have had a prayer there, but then (Jermaine) Wiggins' catch put it in legitimate field goal range, and then Adam did it," said Belichick. "Adam's been a clutch player for us all year. If you want a guy making the play at the end of the game, it's Adam. He's won three games for us in overtime this year, none tougher than the one against Oakland in four inches of snow. Compared to that one, this was a chip shot."

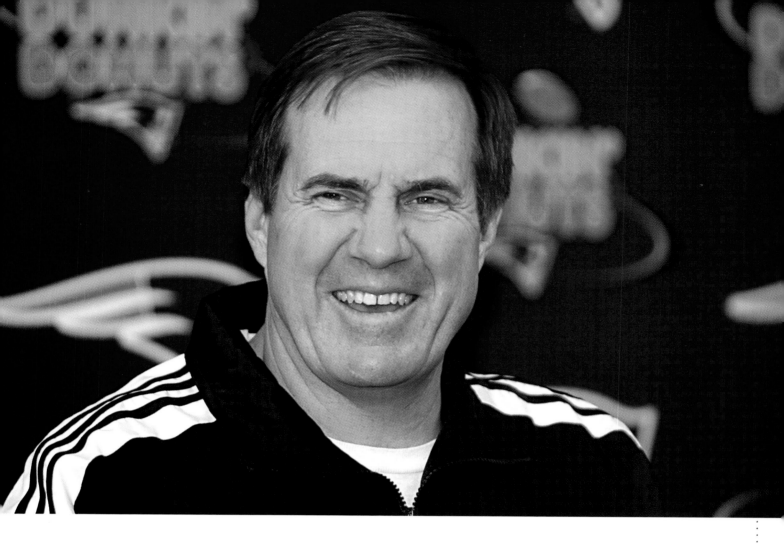

Ten of the 13 points the Patriots' offense put on the board last night in their 20-17 win came in two-minute drills in the waning seconds of the first and second halves, prompting Belichick to reflect, "Maybe we should have done more of it."

And the Pats' lone offensive touchdown—Brady's 8-yard pass to David Patten 31 seconds before halftime—came on a play Belichick and offensive coordinator Charlie Weis had only put into the game plan after watching tapes of the team's final practice session Friday afternoon.

"We'd been running that play as an out, but after looking at the tapes, we realized they'd jump on those outs right away at the goal line, so we changed it to an out-and-up and ran it again," said Belichick. "It was a great call by Charlie and Tom."

This was also the night Brady introduced himself to America. When the Super Bowl MVP goes to Disneyland, they'll probably check his ID. Last night Belichick was asked if he'd ever dreamed the wunderkind quarterback might take his team to the Super Bowl when he first handed him the keys to the car last September. I thought Tom would do a good job with the team, said Belichick. "But remember, at that point we were 0-2. We weren't thinking about the Super Bowl, we were thinking aout trying to win a game. We've come a long way since that point, but back then we were trying to beat the Indianapolis Colts. The Super Bowl was the farthest thing from our minds."

OS VS... NEW ENGLAND PATRIOTS VS. DENVER BRONCOS VS. NEW ENGL.

GAME SEVEN
10.28.01

BRADY'S INT BARRAGE
SEALS LOSS TO BRONCOS

Michael Felger; Boston Herald

The air in Denver may be thin, but it wasn't thin enough to keep Tom Brady in the stratosphere or prevent the Patriots from crashing back to earth yesterday.

Both happened at Invesco Field, as Brady finally acted his age in throwing four fourth-quarter interceptions and the Pats showed they aren't quite ready to win back-to-back games on the road against superior opponents. It all added up to a 31-20 loss to the Broncos and an end to the Pats' modest two-game winning streak.

Afterward, the Pats said the confidence in Brady remains high. Someone who didn't even play put it best.

"I believe in (Brady) totally and the team believes in him totally," Drew Bledsoe said. "He has to come back next week and play better. This team is behind him now as much as ever."

Said Brady: "It's real easy when things go well. This is the hard part. This will be hard to get over, but we have to get over it."

The Pats (3-4) have one more stop on their three-game road swing, and a win in Atlanta next week would put them in decent shape to contend for a playoff berth with half the season remaining. A loss and all bets are off.

Meanwhile, the talk-show debate should swing in a new direction this week, as the Pats had the ball four times in the fourth quarter and Brady threw it to the wrong team every time. But a closer look at the game will also show a defense that couldn't stop the big play.

"(The defense) needs to start contributing more so this young offense can develop," said safety Lawyer Milloy. "We can't put them in adverse situations. We put (Brady) in that situation. When he's stress-free, he's second to none."

The Pats' receivers also shouldered some of the blame, especially veteran Troy Brown, who said he ran the wrong route on Brady's third interception, which led to a 39-yard touchdown return by Denard Walker with 2:24 to go.

"He was reading for the (defensive back) to do one thing and I did another. I screwed it up," said Brown, who also had a few drops. "My expectations are that I'll make those plays."

Added coach Bill Belichick: "We had our chances. We needed one good drive to get the ball in the end zone and we just couldn't get it done. There are a couple of plays we'd all like to have back. But overall (Brady) played well."

It was a back-and-forth game from the opening whistle. With the score tied at 10, things got interesting toward the end of the first half when the Pats got the ball after a Tedy Bruschi interception. Brady then hit Brown with an easy 5-yard scoring pass to make it 17-10. The Pats made it a 10-point game early in the second half when a Matt Stevens interception led to a 44-yard Adam Vinatieri field goal.

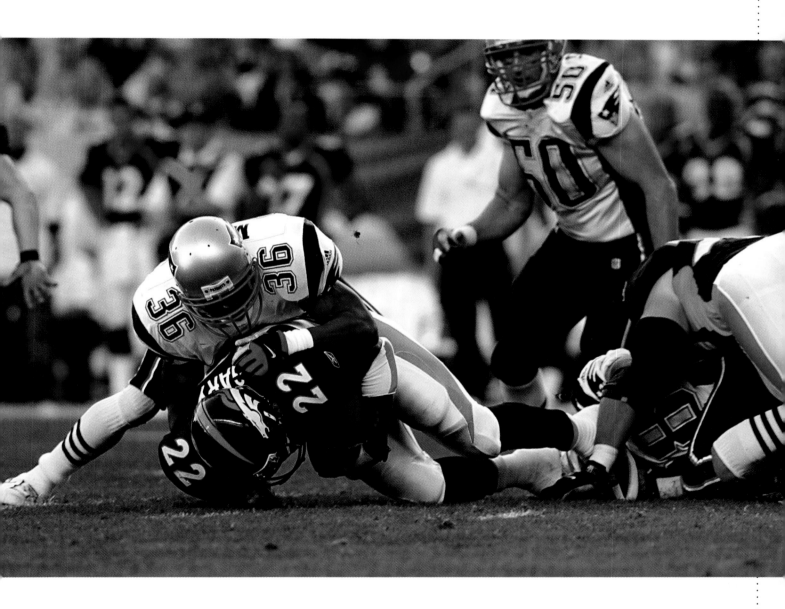

The lead was short-lived, however, as Rod Smith outraced the Pats secondary on a 65-yard scoring play on the next drive and Dwayne Carswell hauled in an 8-yard pass to put the Broncos ahead 24-20. The Smith touchdown was particularly irksome, as a mixup in the Pats' secondary (presumably between Otis Smith and Lawyer Milloy) allowed him to race down the sideline.

"To have two veterans bust a communication, that's unacceptable. Inexcusable," Milloy said. "It's not that we weren't playing hard, it's just the fundamental things have to be corrected if we want to be a good team."

Brady, who had been flawless during his first four games, then started giving the ball away. His first interception in 163 professional attempts came at a very bad time as he missed David Patten in the end zone and Eric Brown made the pick. On the next series, Brady badly overthrew Patten on third-and-2, and this time Deltha O'Neal came up with the ball. The Pats were able to hold a few more times, but Brady couldn't take advantage.

Still, the Pats felt they could have won.

"We can definitely (beat them)," said center Damien Woody. "We moved the ball. It wasn't one of those things where they shut us down. Even though we lost we feel pretty good because we know we could have won. We just can't shoot ourselves in the foot."

The Pats seemed to be building confidence as a team heading into the game. And in a good sign, it seemed to still be there when the final whistle blew.

"We have to throw this game out the window," Milloy said, "because we have a good team."

" I believe in (Brady) totally and the team believes in him totally. He has to come back next week and play better. This team is behind him now as much as ever. "

PATRIOTS QUARTERBACK DREW BLEDSOE

	1st	2nd	3rd	4th	Final
New England	10	7	3	0	20
Denver	7	3	14	7	31

SCORING SUMMARY

Qtr	Team	Play		Time
1st	**PATRIOTS** FG	Vinatieri 24-yd.	....	9:06
1st	**PATRIOTS** TD	Patten 30-yd. pass from Brady (Vinatieri kick)	......	4:57
1st	**BRONCOS** TD	Anderson 8-yd. run (Elam kick)	....	0:57
2nd	**BRONCOS** FG	Elam 50-yd.	....	4:03
2nd	**PATRIOTS** TD	Brown 5-yd. pass from Brady (Vinatieri kick)	......	1:21
3rd	**PATRIOTS** FG	Vinatieri 44-yd.	....	10:59
3rd	**BRONCOS** TD	Smith 65-yd. pass from Griese (Elam kick)	....	10:35
3rd	**BRONCOS** TD	Carswell 8-yd. pass from Griese (Elam kick)	....	3:35
4th	**BRONCOS** TD	Walker 39-yd. interception return (Elam kick)	.....	2:24

OFFENSE

PATRIOTS

PASSING	ATT	COMP	YDS	INT	TD
Brady	38	25	203	4	2
Patten	1	0	0	1	0

RECEIVING	ATT		YDS		TD
Brown	9		86		1
Patten	5		62		1
Faulk	4		26		0
Johnson	2		11		0
Smith	2		11		0
Edwards	1		6		0
Jackson	1		4		0
Redmond	1		-3		0

RUSHING	ATT		YDS		TD
Smith	12		56		0
Brown	1		31		0
Patten	1		13		0
Faulk	5		12		0
Edwards	2		6		0
Redmond	1		0		0
Brady	2		-1		0

BRONCOS

PASSING	ATT	COMP	YDS	INT	TD
Griese	30	19	283	2	2

RECEIVING	ATT		YDS		TD
Smith	6		159		1
Clark	6		94		0
Carswell	3		21		1
Montgomery	2		15		0
Hape	1		0		0

RUSHING	ATT		YDS		TD
Anderson	14		40		1
Gary	10		37		0
Kennison	1		10		0
Griese	4		-1		0

SUPER BOWL CHAMPIONS

PATRIOTS BOUNCE FALCONS
FLUKE TD LEADS TO 24-10 VICTORY

Michael Felger; Boston Herald

The pass from Tom Brady floated through the air, wobbling as it made its way into triple coverage and certain disaster. As Patriots fans held their breath, Troy Brown kept his head. The ball, which was intended for David Patten, hit a body and deflected backward, and Brown snatched it up and sprinted 44 yards for a score.

The play left Brady grabbing his helmet, Drew Bledsoe laughing into his headset and the Patriots feeling like things could finally be going their way.

"Just the way we drew it up," a smiling Belichick said. "The immaculate reception—at least the Patriots version of it."

Belichick had reason to smile. His surging team completed a three-game road swing with a 24-10 victory over the Atlanta Falcons yesterday, giving the Patriots wins in two of those games and a .500 record (4-4) at the season's midpoint.

With five of their last eight games at home, the slate is now set for the Pats to make a run at their first playoff berth since 1998.

"Do I think this is a playoff team? Heck, yeah," Pats center Damien Woody said. "I feel that way and I don't think we've even played our best game yet. But we're definitely in a good spot with 5-of-8 at home. We just have to take advantage."

Belichick said earlier this season that the Pats had to prove they could win consistenly on the road. They've done that. Now comes the hard part: putting together a run that will land them in the postseason.

"It's not about where we are," Belichick said. "It's about where we're going."

Yesterday's game was far from perfect (the Pats committed seven penalties and fumbled the ball away twice), but the Pats did just enough things to come out on top.

Start with the defense, which broke out of a recent slump to register nine sacks and control the line of scrimmage for much of the day. The return of rookie Richard Seymour (sack), the continued resurgence of Willie McGinest (five tackles, two sacks) and the hard hitting of Lawyer Milloy (six tackles, sack) were the key elements to an aggressive game plan devised by defensive coordinator Romeo Crennel.

The Pats put aside the "bend but don't break" philosophy, and the results were impressive. Falcons quarterback Chris Chandler (ribs) was knocked out of the game after six sacks and the fleet-footed Michael Vick (three sacks) fared no better.

"A lot of guys stepped up to play good team defense," Belichick said. "We really rallied to the ball. We wanted to mix in some pressure, and I felt Romeo did a good job of that. . . . (McGinest) coupled with Seymour—it's good to see them out there making plays."

Offensively, the Pats went in believing they could run, and they did. The result was 117 yards on the ground for Antowain Smith, the Pats' first 100-yard rushing day since Dec. 26, 1999.

SUPER BOWL CHAMPIONS

Meanwhile, Brady responded to his first professional adversity. After throwing four fourth-quarter interceptions in Denver last week, Brady came back with three touchdowns and no interceptions yesterday. If Brady is anything, it's confident. One bad quarter was not about to deter him.

"It would take a lot of bad games to get my confidence down," he said. "That's just the way I am— unfortunately, I guess."

Two of Brady's touchdown passes were conventional (a 4-yard fade pattern to Kevin Faulk and a 15-yard swing pass to wide-open fullback Marc Edwards), but the third was far from it. Brown was asked what he was thinking when the ball popped up in the air.

"Franco Harris," he said. "I was thinking about that the whole time I was running in to the end zone."

Patten was asked what was going through his head.

"Yes, Lord!" he said. "I thought the play was dead, and then I hear the crowd and Troy is running into the end zone. It was amazing."

The 44-yard touchdown gave the Pats a commanding 24-7 lead with less than a minute left in the third quarter.

About 30 minutes later, Pats owner Bob Kraft and his wife, Myra, stood near the runway shaking hands with the players and, in Myra's case, offering congratulatory kisses. Belichick left the field waving his hands at hundreds of diehard Pats fans left in the stands.

"We're starting to feel good," Milloy said. "We're getting that swagger we haven't had around here the last few years. Even the games we've lost, we've felt pretty good about them. That's the sign of a good team."

SUPER BOWL CHAMPIONS

**"It's not about where we are.
It's about where we're going."**

PATRIOTS COACH BILL BELICHICK

	1st	2nd	3rd	4th	Final
New England	0	17	7	0	24
Atlanta	7	0	0	3	10

SCORING SUMMARY

QTR	TEAM	PLAY	TIME
1st	**FALCONS**	TD Jefferson 19-yd. pass from Chandler (Feely kick)	2:35
2nd	**PATRIOTS**	TD Faulk 4-yd. pass from Brady (Vinatieri kick)	9:00
2nd	**PATRIOTS**	FG Vinatieri 48-yd.	4:26
2nd	**PATRIOTS**	TD Edwards 15-yd. pass from Brady (Vinatieri kick)	0:15
3rd	**PATRIOTS**	TD Brown 44-yd. pass from Brady (Vinatieri kick) ..	0:34
4th	**FALCONS**	FG Feely 20-yd.	11:28

OFFENSE

PATRIOTS

PASSING	ATT	COMP	YDS	INT	TD
Brady	31	21	250	0	3

RECEIVING	ATT	YDS	TD
Brown	5	99	1
Patten	3	40	0
Smith	3	28	0
Edwards	2	27	1
Faulk	5	21	1
Wiggins	1	16	0
Jackson	1	12	0
Johnson	1	7	0

RUSHING	ATT	YDS	TD
Smith	23	117	0
Edwards	6	11	0
Brown	1	5	0
Faulk	1	2	0
Brady	3	0	0

FALCONS

PASSING	ATT	COMP	YDS	INT	TD
Chandler	20	8	95	1	1
Vick	9	2	56	0	0

RECEIVING	ATT	YDS	TD
Finneran	1	50	0
Martin	3	49	0
Crumpler	2	20	0
Jefferson	1	19	1
Christian	2	15	0
Mathis	1	-2	0

RUSHING	ATT	YDS	TD
Smith	16	84	0
Vick	2	50	0
Chandler	1	6	0

SUPER BOWL CHAMPIONS

LAW PICKS UP PATS

LAW PICKS UP PATS

LAW PICKS UP PATS

LAW PICKS UP PATS

Gus Martins; Boston Herald

With his 21-month-old daughter, Tya, perched firmly on his lap, Ty Law calmly but triumphantly basked in the glow of destiny he believed anchored the Patriots to a 20-17 victory over the St. Louis Rams last night in Super Bowl XXXVI.

The championship, the first ever in the team's 42-year history, came as a perfectly staged bit of redemption for the Patriots, who had lost two previous Super Bowls in the Superdome and who were enormous underdogs in last night's game.

"Believe me, we knew we could win this football game," Law said. "There was no doubt in anybody's mind in that locker room. I thought it was somewhat of a destiny to come down here back to New Orleans.

"We had a couple of subpar seasons after that Super Bowl (in 1997), and the next thing you know we were back here where the unfinished business was at, and we came down here and we played hard when no one would give us a chance."

Law certainly put effort over style last night. He had a team-high eight tackles (seven unassisted), defended two passes and snagged a crucial 47-yard interception he returned for a touchdown to give the Patriots a 7-3 lead with 8:49 remaining in the second quarter.

Playing primarily man-to-man against the Rams' explosive receiving corps, Law said everything broke perfectly, allowing for the interception.

"I have to give a lot of credit to my guys up front," he said. "They were putting a lot of pressure on (Rams quarterback Kurt) Warner all day. On that particular play, we were on a bump-and-run and Isaac Bruce went in motion, so I knew the ball was going to have to come out fast. Luckily, Mike Vrabel went and put pressure on Kurt, and I ran the route just as good as Isaac on that play. The ball was thrown a little behind, and I saw an opportunity and I wasn't going to let a 300-pound lineman catch me."

SUPER BOWL CHAMPIONS

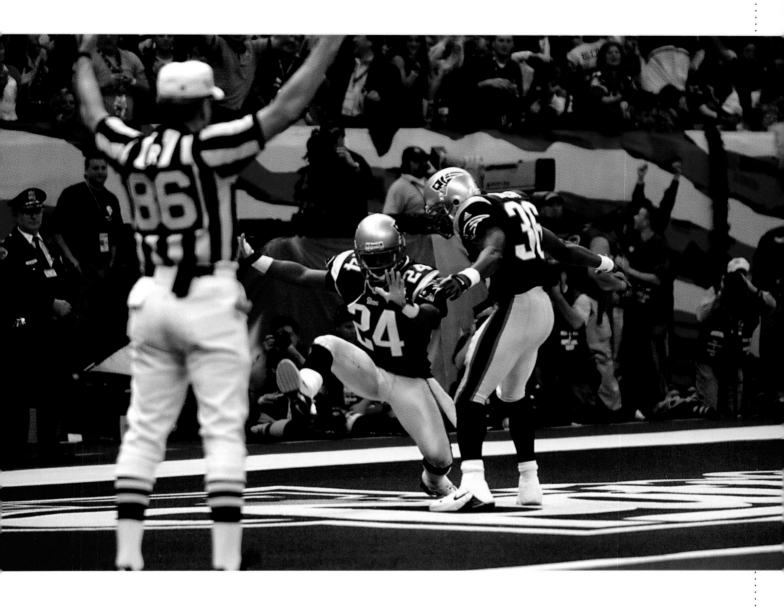

Law admitted that if he was a betting man without the inside information to the Patriots' psyche, he'd have put his money on St. Louis last night.

"Everyone talked about the St. Louis Rams track team," he said. "But I've never seen anyone win a gold medal at the Olympics with someone standing in their lane. We were standing in their lane (last night).

"We played physical and we were the better team."

While lavishing praise on the Rams, Law said his team's achievement last night was paralleled by only one other moment in his life.

"They came back and had a great run and almost put the game in overtime," he said. "But we were a little more resilient today, and I'd like to say that other than my daughter being born this is the greatest feeling I've ever had in my life."

PATS SURVIVE SCARE
FROM BILLS

Michael Felger; Boston Herald

The Patriots escaped the trap and put up another win yesterday. That's about the only nice thing you can say about their mistake-filled, 21-11 victory over Buffalo at blustery Foxboro Stadium.

Now, with the Pats at 5-4 and squarely in the mix for a playoff berth, everyone will turn their attention elsewhere and start praying for the one thing that will help the Pats on Sunday night when they host the high-octane St. Louis Rams in a nationally televised showdown:

Snow.

How hot are the Pats? We'll find out soon, as Kurt Warner, Marshall Faulk and the Super Bowl champions from two seasons ago will come to town after putting up 48 points in a win over Carolina yesterday. In the Pats locker room, the words "St. Louis Rams" were on the lips of more than one player.

"Best team in football," said center Damien Woody. "We have to step our game up. We can't play like we did (yesterday) or we'll get our asses kicked in prime time."

Woody's frank comment was not meant to convey that the Pats were upset with yesterday's result. In fact, coach Bill Belichick and most of his players seemed pleased that they were able to move above .500 (for the first time since 1999's Week 13, when the Pats were 7-6) while playing far from their best game against a traditionally tough division opponent. It's just that everyone realized it will take more on Sunday.

Either that, or the Pats will need a nor'easter.

"We're not backing down to the challenge," said quarterback Tom Brady, who raised his record as a starter to 5-2 despite an up-and-down performance. "If you want to be the best you have to beat the best."

Yesterday's win belonged to the defense, which came up with five sacks, two turnovers and several key stops. Much like last week in Atlanta, the Pats blitzed early and often, and Bills quarterback Rob Johnson was gone by the end of the fourth quarter with a shoulder injury.

Finally, the defense carried the offense. While Ted Johnson and Richard Seymour were recording seven tackles each, Brady was throwing for just 107 yards while being intercepted once and sacked seven times. The offense committed three turnovers and the team was flagged for seven penalties for 75 yards.

Belichick took most of the blame for the sloppiness, saying, "from a coaching standpoint I don't think it was my best job." But Belichick also took the stance that a win is a win.

"We lacked the consistency we'd really like to have, but you have to recognize Buffalo (1-7) has a much better team than their record indicates," said the coach. "We've had games like this where we've had lapses and mistakes and lost. It's good to get one."

Belichick's comments notwithstanding, the Bills were awful. They were sloppy on offense and

penalty-prone everywhere. The Bills were flagged nine times for 75 yards on the day, several of which led directly to Patriots points. The most egregious came in the third quarter when a pass interference penalty on Antoine Winfield in the end zone set up a 1-yard scoring plunge by Antowain Smith. That put the Pats firmly in control at 14-3. Brady had given the Pats a 7-0 lead in the first quarter on a pretty 6-yard fade pass to Kevin Faulk.

Meanwhile, Smith, going against his old team, hit the century mark again with 20 rushes for 100 yards and two scores. His 42-yard touchdown late in the fourth quarter sealed the win. The Bills had drawn to within three points just seconds earlier after a Brady fumble set up a 17-yard scoring pass from Rob Johnson's replacement, Alex Van Pelt, to Peerless Price.

The Pats know they need to be better.

"We need to be better next week," said Mike Vrabel, who recovered a crucial onside kick following the Price touchdown. "You can't swim until you get up above the water, and now we've done that. We're going to enjoy this win. They're hard to come by in this league."

Ted Johnson was asked if yesterday's effort will be good enough next week.

"No, obviously" said Johnson. "We have the best team in the NFL coming in here. The defense is going to have to have its best game. We have to come up with something to shut them down."

Belichick has developed a reputation over the years for doing just that against some of the best offenses in football. All eyes will be on him to see what he comes up with this week.

We've had games like this where we've had lapses and mistakes and lost. It's good to get one.

PATRIOTS COACH BILL BELICHICK

	1st	2nd	3rd	4th	Final
Buffalo	0	3	0	8	11
New England	7	0	7	7	21

SCORING SUMMARY

Qtr	Team	Play		Time
1st	**PATRIOTS**	TD	Faulk 6-yd. pass from Brady (Vinatieri kick)	3:09
2nd	**BILLS**	FG	Arians 24-yd.	11:38
3rd	**PATRIOTS**	TD	A. Smith 1-yd. run (Vinatieri kick)	7:27
4th	**BILLS**	TD	Price 17-yd. pass from Van Pelt (2-pt. conv. succeeds)	2:43
4th	**PATRIOTS**	TD	A. Smith 42-yd. run (Vinatieri kick)	1:52

OFFENSE

PATRIOTS

PASSING	ATT	COMP	YDS	INT	TD
Brady	21	15	107	1	1

RECEIVING	ATT	YDS	TD
Faulk	7	29	1
Patten	1	26	0
Brown	2	25	0
Edwards	3	17	0
Johnson	1	6	0
Wiggins	1	4	0

RUSHING	ATT	YDS	TD
Smith	20	100	2
Brown	1	17	0
Edwards	3	8	0
Patten	1	7	0
Faulk	2	3	0
Brady	4	-1	0

BILLS

PASSING	ATT	COMP	YDS	INT	TD
Johnson	26	14	167	1	0
Van Pelt	7	2	37	1	1

RECEIVING	ATT	YDS	TD
Germany	4	69	0
Price	3	59	1
Riemersma	1	36	0
Centers	3	30	0
Moulds	3	7	0
Black	1	4	0
Henry	1	-1	0

RUSHING	ATT	YDS	TD
Henry	16	51	0
Johnson	5	18	0

SUPER BOWL CHAMPIONS

PATS GIVE AWAY BIG CHANCE

TURNOVERS HELP POWERFUL RAMS QUASH UPSET HOPES

Michael Felger; Boston Herald

Bill Belichick said all week that the Patriots would have to play their best game to beat the St. Louis Rams.

The Pats didn't come close last night, and what they did come up with was not nearly enough to defeat the consensus best team in football. The result was a 24-17 loss and a drop back to the .500 mark for the 5-5 Patriots.

On an evening that was far too gentle as far as the Pats were concerned (game-time temperature of 49 degrees with light winds), Kurt Warner and the Rams were mistake-prone yet deadly when they had to be. And as many mistakes as the Rams (four turnovers) made, the Patriots' miscues (three turnovers) were far more costly.

"You can't turn the ball over to those guys," said quarterback Tom Brady, who could hear Drew Bledsoe's name a lot more this week after an uneven performance that included a key third-quarter interception. "On offense we were really moving the ball—it's not like they stopped us."

The Patriots took care of that themselves.

Afterward, the play everyone pointed to was an Antowain Smith fumble at the end of the first half, one that resulted in a 14-point swing on the scoreboard. The Pats were leading, 10-7, when Smith was stripped at the Rams' 1-yard line. The Pats challenged, but replays were inconclusive. Eight plays later, Warner hit Marshall Faulk from 11 yards out and the Rams had a lead they wouldn't give up.

"I look at the outcome of the game, and I can't do anything but blame myself for losing the game," said Smith.

Belichick felt Smith was down before he fumbled, but the coach also realized that was far from the only mistake. The Pats' three giveaways led directly to 17 Rams points.

"There were plenty of other plays in the game," said Belichick. "And we just didn't have enough of them."

Despite the result, the Pats felt they could have—and should have—won.

"For sure," said receiver Troy Brown. "We just made a few crucial mistakes and it crushed us."

Added Brady (19-of-27, 185 yards, two interceptions): "That's a (8-1) football team and we were right there with them. They're supposed to be Super Bowl champs and we're in the game."

Defensively, it was a mixed bag. On one hand, the defense was directly responsible for 10 points thanks to a 52-yard interception return for a touchdown from Terrell Buckley and a Tedy Bruschi pick that set up an Adam Vinatieri field goal.

But the defense also failed at crucial junctures. The most glaring was the Rams' 97-yard drive at the end of the half, but there were other big moments as well. None was bigger than late in the fourth quarter.

Brady had just hit David Patten with a 10-yard touchdown pass to make it a seven-point game with

7:46 remaining. That's when the defense needed to step up, stop the Rams and give Brady and the offense one more chance. Instead, the Rams picked up four first downs and ran out the clock.

Schematically, the Pats blitzed Warner with only occasional effectiveness. Otherwise, they sat back and watched as Warner (401 yards, three touchdowns) and his lightning-quick stable of receivers stretched the field and caught pass after pass. When Isaac Bruce (seven catches, 130 yards) or Torry Holt (seven catches, 89 yards) weren't torching the Pats, Faulk was.

The Rams' stellar running back was the star of the game, with 83 rushing yards, 70 receiving yards and several huge plays on third downs.

"I know why we lost," said cornerback Ty Law, who had a particularly tough time with the Rams' speed. "We made enough plays to win, but they made more. We have to blame ourselves. They're a great team, and I don't want to take anything away from them, but a lot of it was that we just beat ourselves."

The Pats and Brady likely face a make-or-break game this week against New Orleans. A win and the Pats are still in the playoff hunt. A loss and the Pats' chances—along with Brady's starting job—could be in jeopardy.

"We made enough plays to win, but they made more. We have to blame ourselves. They're a great team, and I don't want to take anything away from them, but a lot of it was that we just beat ourselves."

PATRIOTS CORNERBACK TY LAW

	1st	2nd	3rd	4th	Final
St. Louis	7	7	3	7	24
New England	7	3	0	7	17

SCORING SUMMARY

Qtr	Team	Play		Time
1st	**RAMS**	TD	Holt 16-yd. pass from Warner (Wilkins kick)	9:38
1st	**PATRIOTS**	TD	Buckley 52-yd. interception return (Vinatieri kick)	1:55
2nd	**PATRIOTS**	FG	Vinatieri 33-yd.	14:06
2nd	**RAMS**	TD	Faulk 9-yd. pass from Warner (Wilkins kick)	0:31
3rd	**RAMS**	FG	Wilkins 35-yd.	3:06
4th	**RAMS**	TD	Hodgins 11-yd. pass from Warner (Wilkins kick)	10:32
4th	**PATRIOTS**	TD	Patten 10-yd. pass from Brady (Vinatieri kick)	7:46

OFFENSE

RAMS

PASSING	ATT	COMP	YDS	INT	TD
Warner	42	30	401	2	3

RECEIVING	ATT	YDS	TD
Bruce	7	130	0
Holt	7	89	1
Faulk	7	70	1
Proehl	5	62	0
Robinson	2	27	0
Conwell	1	12	0
Hodgins	1	11	1

RUSHING	ATT	YDS	TD
Faulk	20	83	0
Warner	6	3	0
Canidate	1	1	0
Conwell	1	-1	0

PATRIOTS

PASSING	ATT	COMP	YDS	INT	TD
Brady	27	19	185	2	1

RECEIVING	ATT	YDS	TD
Brown	8	91	0
Patten	2	37	1
Faulk	3	19	0
Rutledge	2	16	0
Johnson	2	11	0
Edwards	1	6	0
Smith	1	5	0

RUSHING	ATT	YDS	TD
Smith	15	36	0
Faulk	2	7	0
Brady	2	6	0
Edwards	1	2	0

LEADING BY EXAMPLE

LEADING BY EXAMPLE

LEADING BY EXAMPLE

LEADING BY EXAMPLE

Michael O'Connor; Boston Herald

When Lawyer Milloy is asked what he can teach to the younger Patriots players about preparing for the playoffs, his answer is likely to be in the form of another, semi-annoyed, question: "What, do I look like some kind of camp counselor to you?"

In other words, the six-year veteran believes that his teammates—who've helped get the Pats this far—are all professionals, no matter how long they've been in the league.

Even rookies should know how to prepare for big games against big-time opponents, like last night's battle against the Raiders at Foxboro Stadium.

The veteran's job is to be a role model, not a babysitter, and lead by example, Milloy said; let the less-experienced players figure it out for themselves.

Show, don't tell.

And the Pro Bowl safety believes most of his fellow vets feel the same way about bringing the younger players along—especially at this critical time of the season.

"We really haven't said anything to them, haven't said anything at all to them," he said. "You're really trying just to kind of lead by example.

"At practice, or whatever, you don't say, 'Come on, (first-year player Richard) Seymour, you have to pick it up' or '(first-year starter Tom) Brady, don't throw that pass.' We just pick the pass off and he knows then he shouldn't do that," Milloy said with a soft chuckle.

But it's not so much about nurturing the Patriots youth movement as it is making sure his performance rises a notch or two— and make that the standard for everyone.

As the playoffs loomed, he said, "We pick our level of intensity up during practice and we challenge the younger guys to pick their own level of competition up."

And they knew they would have to, if they planned to beat the Raiders, who've relied successfully on some flashy pass routes from Rich Gannon & Co.

SUPER BOWL CHAMPIONS

"It's going to be about good communication, first and foremost," Milloy said. "The West Coast teams use some shifts to get you that one step behind, so we're preparing for that. It's a bit like a chess game."

No matter what team or what sort of offense they face, it's all about effort and focus, Milloy said. And that's what the most important lesson is for their less-experienced teammates.

"We're out there flying around and doing our thing and that's how you lead by example, not by saying or explaining to everybody what to expect," he said. "You just kind of let it happen naturally."

PATS MARCH BY SAINTS
BRADY'S FOUR TD PASSES KEY TO VICTORY

Michael Felger; Boston Herald

Bill Belichick didn't need to look at the game film and he didn't need to consult with his assistants.

"I think it's pretty clear-cut," the Patriots coach said.

Yes it is. Tom Brady is the quarterback of the Patriots. And if the team continues to play as it did yesterday, a playoff berth should be well within reach.

With their season at a crossroads, Brady and the Pats made a statement against the New Orleans Saints at damp, rainy Foxboro Stadium. Brady showed the starting quarterback job is in its rightful place and the Pats showed they can be a team to be reckoned with. It all added up to a resounding, wire-to-wire, 34-17 victory over the Saints.

"I told the players it was a tremendous win," said Belichick, whose team will take a 6-5 record into a key matchup at the AFC East-leading New York Jets next week. "I thought they played their best game of the year."

And just in time, too. A loss and the Pats would probably have been a longshot playoff contender while Brady would be in jeopardy of losing his job. Instead, the Pats and Brady are right where they need to be with just more than a month left in the season.

The key was the offense, which rebounded from a couple of uneven games to move the ball and put points on the board. Brady (258 yards, four touchdowns) was fabulous, running back Antowain Smith (111 yards) had his best game as a Patriot and receiver David Patten continued to draw key pass interference calls to set up touchdowns.

"Tom was hot, but it was a combination of everything," said center Damien Woody, who keyed a solid effort by the Pats' offensive line. "Now we've got to keep it going. I'm sick of these single wins here and there. It's crunch time now. We've got to string some things together."

Defensively, it was back to a bend-but-don't-break philosophy. Saints quarterback Aaron Brooks threw for 307 yards and ran for another 65, but running back Ricky Williams (56 yards on 15 carries) wasn't a huge factor and the Saints consistently bogged down in the red zone. The Pats, by contrast, scored touchdowns on all three trips inside the Saints' 20.

Pats safety Lawyer Milloy didn't play up near the line of scrimmage as expected, but he was still a huge factor, recording a team-high 10 tackles while recording one interception and two passes defended. Milloy's physical play was symbolic of the effort put forth by the entire Pats defense. The Pats read a lot about how the Saints considered themselves a tough team and the Pats took that as a challenge.

"They did a lot of talking about how physical they were," said Tedy Bruschi, who played well in place of Ted Johnson at middle linebacker. "Well, they can keep talking about it on the plane."

SUPER BOWL CHAMPIONS

As for Smith, the sad memory of fumbling near the goal line against the St. Louis Rams last week was a motivating factor.

"I feel like I cost us the game last week," said Smith, who ran with authority all game. "So I really wanted to do something to come out and bounce back."

Earlier in the week, Belichick announced Brady as the starter over Drew Bledsoe, in part, because he wanted the focus to be on Brady during practice. Belichick said that paid off yesterday, as Brady hit several plays during the game that were run successfully last week.

"When you're able to run and play-action pass, we're pretty tough to stop. That's our game," Brady said. "We're starting to really come into our own. It's the kind of stuff we have to build on, the kind of stuff we have to continue to do if we want to stay in the race."

The Pats dominated the first half, scoring 20 unanswered points on three Brady touchdown passes. The first was a perfectly designed, 41-yard screen to Smith. The second was an 8-yard touch pass to tightly covered Troy Brown. The third was a pretty, 24-yard strike to Charles Johnson over the middle with seconds remaining in the half.

Brooks and the Saints made some noise in the second half, but a short touchdown pass from Brady to Marc Edwards and a 3-yard run by Smith snuffed out any hope of a comeback.

Now it's on to the Meadowlands, where the Pats will once again have something to prove.

"We all know what kind of game that's going to be," the ever-confident Brady said. "I like our chances."

" **I told the players it was a tremendous win. I thought they played their best game of the year.** "

PATRIOTS COACH BILL BELICHICK

	1st	2nd	3rd	4th	Final
New Orleans	0	0	10	7	17
New England	7	13	0	14	34

SCORING SUMMARY

Qtr	Team	Play		Time
1st	**PATRIOTS**	TD	A. Smith 41-yd. pass from Brady (Vinatieri kick) .	11:35
2nd	**PATRIOTS**	TD	Brown 8-yd. pass from Brady (2-pt. conv. failed) ...	7:23
2nd	**PATRIOTS**	TD	Johnson 24-yd. pass from Brady (Vinatieri kick)	0:10
3rd	**SAINTS**	FG	Carney 31-yd.	6:59
3rd	**SAINTS**	TD	Williams 3-yd. run (Carney kick)	2:11
4th	**PATRIOTS**	TD	Edwards 2-yd. pass from Brady (Vinatieri kick) ...	13:24
4th	**SAINTS**	TD	Jackson 7-yd. pass from Brooks (Carney kick)	8:15
4th	**PATRIOTS**	TD	A. Smith 3-yd. run (Vinatieri kick)	2:25

OFFENSE

PATRIOTS

PASSING	ATT	COMP	YDS	INT	TD
Brady	26	19	258	0	4

RECEIVING	ATT	YDS	TD
Brown	7	91	1
Patten	3	47	0
Johnson	2	44	1
Smith	3	42	1
Edwards	3	30	1
Wiggins	1	4	0

RUSHING	ATT	YDS	TD
Smith	24	111	1
Faulk	3	36	0
Redmond	4	20	0
Brady	4	14	0
Edwards	3	10	0

SAINTS

PASSING	ATT	COMP	YDS	INT	TD
Brooks	39	16	307	2	1

RECEIVING	ATT	YDS	TD
Horn	4	97	0
Jackson	5	78	1
Connell	2	49	0
Williams	2	44	0
Williams	3	39	0

RUSHING	ATT	YDS	TD
Brooks	7	65	0
Williams	15	56	1

PATS TAKE A HUGE STEP
RALLY TO BEAT JETS

Michael Felger; Boston Herald

Curtis Martin couldn't believe it. The 78,712 fans at Giants Stadium couldn't believe it. About the only people who believed it were along the Patriots' sideline, where jubilation reigned following the Pats' stunning, come-from-behind, 17-16 win over the New York Jets yesterday.

"I don't mean to sound arrogant, but I'm still in awe of the fact we lost," said Martin, the stellar Jets running back whose last season with the Pats (1997) marked the last time anyone in New England had reason to believe. "Nothing in my entire mind could figure this out."

Actually, it's not that hard. The Patriots are a new team with a new quarterback and a new attitude. If the postseason were to begin today, the Pats (7-5) would be in. Gone are the bad vibes from the Pete Carroll era and the frustrations from last year's 5-11 record. In their place are confidence, resiliency and momentum. The Pats are starting to use the "P" word.

"This was a playoff game," safety Lawyer Milloy said. "We're already in playoff mode. We're trying to stay humble. We haven't clinched anything yet, so we know we have a lot of work to do. We don't have a cocky team. But the thing is that we know we have a good team. A lot of the guys are starting to believe."

Think this game meant something to coach Bill Belichick? The Pats' normally subdued coach went wild (for him) in the closing seconds of the win, pumping his fists and slapping helmets. It was just over two years ago that he turned his back on the Jets and took the head job with the Pats.

"I thought we had a real courageous effort," Belichick said. "We really hung in there and fought back. I'm really proud of them. We're 7-5 and a lot of people didn't think we'd be in this position. We came from a long way back, a long way uphill, and it's pretty satisfying."

Linebacker Bryan Cox said the game was "a tale of two halves" and he couldn't have been more correct. The Pats were simply awful in the first 30 minutes, as they were dominated in the trenches and on the scoreboard. The Jets led 13-0 at the intermission, but it could have been 130-0. The Pats looked dead in the water.

In the second half, the Pats defense stepped up and created turnovers and quarterback Tom Brady and the offense adjusted. The result was 17 second-half points—the final three coming on a 28-yard Adam Vinatieri field goal with 6:29 remaining—and a huge win against a bitter rival.

Several players and coaches stood up and spoke to the team during the halftime break. Cox, Brady and center Damien Woody all said a few words and offensive coordinator Charlie Weis also had a say. The messages worked.

"The coaches got up a bit," fullback Marc Edwards said. "We looked at each other like, 'That first half is not us. That's not who we are.' "

SUPER BOWL CHAMPIONS

Said Woody: "It was a wake-up call. A lot of people stepped up. And that's what this team is all about."

Cox provided his own inspiration, suiting up for the game just a month after breaking his leg in two places.

"That was a great win for us," Cox said. "We needed to come up here and win this kind of game. I think it built some character."

The Pats' coaches made several adjustments at halftime, none more crucial than in the passing game. With Jets defensive backs Aaron Glenn and Ray Mickens down with injuries, Weis had Brady go to short drops and quick passes. Brady, who took a beating in the first half, was masterful in the second, completing 15-of-17 passes.

A pair of key third-down conversions—a 46-yard pass to little-used receiver Fred Coleman and a 40-yard pass to Antowain Smith—set up touchdown runs from Smith and Edwards. The defense got big plays from Roman Phifer (team-high nine tackles), Richard Seymour (1 1/2 sacks) and Mike Vrabel (interception).

Terrell Buckley's fourth-down interception at the Pats' 33-yard line with just over two minutes remaining sealed the win. A gutsy quarterback keeper by Brady a minute later killed the clock.

Two months ago, the Pats were 0-2 with Drew Bledsoe on the sideline. Now Brady and the Pats are thinking about an AFC East title. They are currently two games behind Miami (8-3) in the loss column and one behind the Jets (7-4).

"You're talking to a team that was 5-11 and now we're 7-5," said Brady. "This was a huge win. Hopefully, this will be a springboard for the rest of the season."

SUPER BOWL CHAMPIONS

"We haven't clinched anything yet, so we know we have a lot of work to do. We don't have a cocky team. But the thing is that we know we have a good team. A lot of the guys are starting to believe."

PATRIOTS SAFETY LAWYER MILLOY

	1st	2nd	3rd	4th	Final
New England	0	0	14	3	17
NY Jets	10	3	3	0	16

SCORING SUMMARY

QTR	TEAM	PLAY	TIME
1st	JETS	TD Coles 34-yd. pass from Testaverde (Hall kick)	11:52
1st	JETS	FG Hall 19-yd.	4:53
2nd	JETS	FG Hall 40-yd.	2:47
3rd	PATRIOTS	TD A. Smith 4-yd. run (Vinatieri kick)	10:19
3rd	JETS	FG Hall 50-yd.	6:57
3rd	PATRIOTS	TD Edwards 4-yd. run (Vinatieri kick)	2:11
4th	PATRIOTS	FG Vinatieri 28-yd.	6:29

OFFENSE

PATRIOTS

PASSING	ATT	COMP	YDS	INT	TD
Brady	28	20	213	0	0

RECEIVING	ATT	YDS	TD
Patten	6	60	0
Brown	8	59	0
Coleman	1	46	0
Smith	3	43	0
Rutledge	1	9	0
Edwards	1	-4	0

RUSHING	ATT	YDS	TD
Smith	12	28	1
Faulk	3	23	0
Redmond	3	17	0
Edwards	2	5	1
Brady	3	0	0

JETS

PASSING	ATT	COMP	YDS	INT	TD
Testaverde	33	19	184	2	1

RECEIVING	ATT	YDS	TD
Coles	3	63	1
Chrebet	5	48	0
Moss	2	40	0
Becht	2	16	0
Martin	5	16	0
Anderson	1	1	0
Dearth	1	0	0

RUSHING	ATT	YDS	TD
Martin	19	87	0
Testaverde	2	21	0
Jordan	2	7	0
Anderson	3	6	0
Coles	1	-2	0

SUPER BOWL CHAMPIONS

BROWN-OUT IN FOXBORO
BELICHICK, PATS HAVE RIGHT TOUCH

Michael Felger; Boston Herald

Foxboro Stadium had been empty for nearly an hour when Bill Belichick walked onto the field with a football and his three young children, Amanda, Stephen and Brian. For the next 20 minutes, reporters up in the pressbox were treated to a Belichick family game of touch football.

"THAT'S Bill Belichick?" asked one incredulous Cleveland writer.

"Total torture," said another.

"Doesn't he have a backyard?" chimed in a third.

Yes, that Bill Belichick and, yes, he does have a backyard. It's called Foxboro Stadium, and with the way things are going, it could be the site of one last playoff game before the wrecking ball comes in February.

The Patriots won, again, yesterday, making just enough plays to beat the Cleveland Browns, 27-16. With an 8-5 record, the Pats remain firmly in the middle of the AFC playoff picture. Given their schedule (three winnable games) and the confidence level in the locker room (very high), the Pats have every reason to believe the AFC East title is within reach.

It's a far cry from Belichick's tumultuous and mostly unsuccessful tenure as coach of the former Browns franchise from 1991-95. And as hard as it may be for people in Cleveland to believe, it's obvious now that Belichick has what it takes to be a winning NFL head coach. His Patriots have won three straight and sit one game behind first-place

Miami (which hosts Indianapolis tonight) in the division race.

Belichick certainly pushed all the right buttons against the Browns. He got two huge plays on special teams after devoting extra practice time to the plays during the week. He got more solid play from his young and improving offensive line. He got another winning effort from his quarterback, Tom Brady, who overcame two costly interceptions to put up his eighth win in 11 starts.

Most of all, Belichick somehow got his players to believe the Browns didn't respect them. Butch Davis' team has developed a brash reputation, and Patriots coaches made sure their players knew what was being said back in Cleveland.

"They're big talkers over there," said cornerback Ty Law. "They said a lot of things in the newspapers over there that we really didn't like. We knew going in that they didn't respect us. It's easy to smack somebody in the mouth in the media, but it looks kind of foolish when you lose."

The game marked the return of Terry Glenn, but the embattled receiver was overshadowed by hard-working teammate Troy Brown, who returned a punt 85 yards for a touchdown and finished with a team-high seven catches for 89 yards.

"I'm more excited about being 8-5," said Brown. "I'm more excited about winning."

As for Brown's second-quarter touchdown, Belichick and special teams coach Brad Seely saw something they liked on the Cleveland game film.

On Thursday, Belichick and Seely had the players put in extra practice time on the middle punt return.

"It really paid off," said Belichick, who watched Brown dodge two tackles and get key blocks from Lawyer Milloy and Richard Seymour before finding paydirt. The score put the Pats ahead to stay at 17-10.

The second big play in the kicking game came in the fourth quarter when Adam Vinatieri's pooch punt out of field goal formation was downed by the Pats at the Cleveland 2-yard line. Jermaine Wiggins made a diving effort to keep the ball out of the end zone, and the advantageous field position eventually resulted in Antowain Smith's game-clinching 5-yard touchdown run with 2:43 left.

"We've been working on that play since the first day of training camp," said Belichick. "It's looked like that in practice nearly every time we've run it."

Meanwhile, Brady threw one interception returned for a touchdown (a 49-yarder to Corey Fuller) and another bad interception that eventually led to a field goal. Otherwise, Brady was solid, completing 19-of-28 passes for 218 yards. Smith (76 yards, two TDs) continued to show a nose for the goal line, while Glenn had four catches for 67 yards.

The defense intercepted Cleveland quarterback Tim Couch three times (Anthony Pleasant, Terrell Buckley and Tebucky Jones). Linebackers Roman Phifer (11 tackles) and Tedy Bruschi (10 tackles) were outstanding as usual.

"Another good team win," said Belichick. "We had a lot of big plays from different people. That's been the formula."

Added center Damien Woody: "I don't think it's the cleanest game we've played. But a win is a win. When people look back at the schedule and they get to Cleveland, all they'll see is a 'W.'"

" **Another good team win. We had a lot of big plays from different people. That's been the formula.** "

PATRIOTS COACH BILL BELICHICK

	1st	2nd	3rd	4th	Final
Cleveland	10	0	3	3	16
New England	3	17	0	7	27

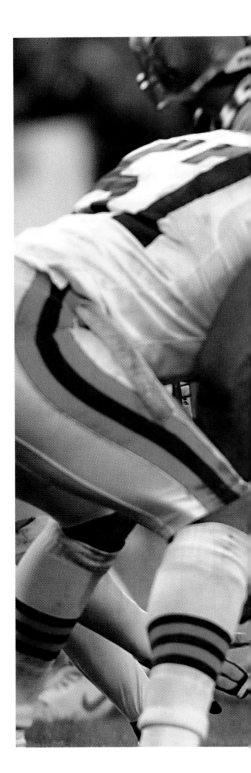

SCORING SUMMARY

Qtr	Team	Play		Time
1st	PATRIOTS	FG	Vinatieri 54-yd.	9:41
1st	BROWNS	FG	Dawson 27-yd.	1:21
1st	BROWNS	TD	Fuller 49-yd. interception return (Dawson kick) ..	1:02
2nd	PATRIOTS	TD	A. Smith 1-yd. run (Vinatieri kick)	9:39
2nd	PATRIOTS	TD	Brown 85-yd. punt return (Vinatieri kick)	3:28
2nd	PATRIOTS	FG	Vinatieri 38-yd.	0:03
3rd	BROWNS	FG	Dawson 39-yd.	10:45
4th	BROWNS	FG	Dawson 22-yd.	12:39
4th	PATRIOTS	TD	A. Smith 5-yd. run (Vinatieri kick)	2:43

OFFENSE

PATRIOTS

PASSING	ATT	COMP	YDS	INT	TD
Brady	28	19	218	2	0

RECEIVING	ATT	YDS	TD
Brown	7	89	0
Glenn	4	67	0
Patten	3	41	0
Faulk	3	11	0
Redmond	1	8	0
Edwards	1	2	0

RUSHING	ATT	YDS	TD
Smith	21	76	2
Patten	1	7	0
Edwards	4	3	0
Faulk	2	0	0
Brown	1	-2	0
Brady	4	-3	0

BROWNS

PASSING	ATT	COMP	YDS	INT	TD
Couch	39	20	244	3	0

RECEIVING	ATT	YDS	TD
Johnson	8	95	0
White	3	57	0
Northcutt	2	29	0
Dawson	2	26	0
Jackson	2	15	0
Santiago	2	11	0
Shea	1	11	0

RUSHING	ATT	YDS	TD
Jackson	16	34	0
Couch	1	9	0
White	2	7	0

SUPER BOWL CHAMPIONS

PATS BOOT BILLS IN OT
VICTORY SETS UP KEY BATTLE WITH MIAMI

Michael Felger; Boston Herald

At some point, someone may have to call a doctor for the Patriots.

The reason?

To have the horseshoe removed from their collective backside.

There appears to be no other diagnosis for a Pats team that won its fourth straight game yesterday—a 12-9 overtime decision over the Bills—thanks largely to a fortuitous bounce and an obscure ruling. That confluence of events, combined with Miami's loss in San Francisco, sets up a Pats-Dolphins game Saturday in Foxboro that will likely determine the champion of the AFC East.

At training camp in July, coach Bill Belichick handed out T- shirts to his players featuring the slogan: "Wanted: Winners." Given the Pats' 5-11 record a year ago, it appeared to be wishful thinking. But after nearly five months in the closet, Belichick brought the shirts out of hibernation and hung them up in the locker room following the game. The Pats (9-5) are now assured of their first winning season since 1998.

"You're going to have to start believing in this team sooner or later," said linebacker Mike Vrabel, moments after Adam Vinatieri's 23-yard chip shot field goal split the uprights at 9:15 of overtime.

The true believers will be put to the test Saturday, when the Dolphins (9-4) come to town to play the biggest football game in New England in some time. While linebacker Bryan Cox said looking ahead to the game was "stupid foolishness," it was on the mind of more than one player.

"It's as big as it gets," said special teams captain Larry Izzo, a former Dolphin. "It's a game you circled when the season started."

Added Lawyer Milloy: "It's big. Everyone can talk about the playoffs, but the No. 1 goal you set the first day of training camp is winning the AFC East. It's what December football is all about."

Meanwhile, the play that everyone will be talking about today occurred on the Pats' first possession of overtime. With the ball on the Pats' 46-yard line, Tom Brady hit David Patten with a 13-yard pass down the sideline. Patten was hit hard by Buffalo's Keion Carpenter. Patten fumbled and Bills cornerback Nate Clements recovered.

The play automatically went to video review, and the outcome seemed obvious: Patten clearly had possession of the ball before fumbling, and Clements clearly recovered in bounds. Buffalo ball, right? Wrong. Referee Mike Carey saw the ball, prior to being recovered, touch Patten's feet while Patten's head was out of bounds. By rule, the ball was dead. Patriots' ball. On the next play, running back Antowain Smith broke loose from a pile of bodies and rumbled 38 yards to set up Vinatieri's game-winner.

Afterward, some claimed knowledge of the rule and others pleaded ignorance. A few players said Belichick showed the team video clips illustrating the rule in training camp. "Leave it to Belichick," said one player. "He thinks of everything."

Personnel director Scott Pioli was apparently not at the film session. He was asked if he knew the rule. "I do now," said Pioli. "Thank you, rule man."

As for the game, it was mostly a lot of field goals (seven) and incomplete passes (38). Neither offense played well, which kept the score close as

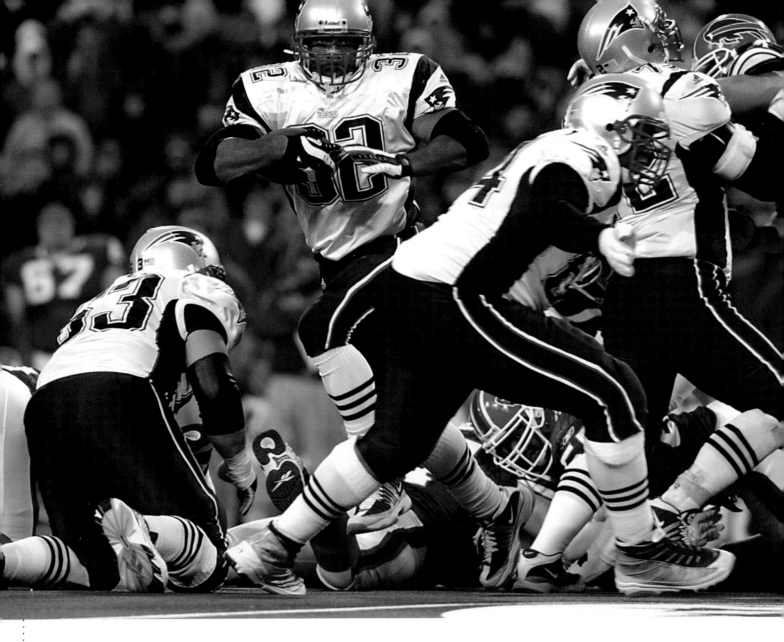

usual. The Pats and Bills have now played into overtime in four of their last five meetings.

There's no other way to say it: It was an ugly win.

"No surprise there," said Belichick. "That's the way these Buffalo-New England games go."

Added Cox: "The thing I tried to explain to the players is that, coming into today, what did you expect? I never feel bad about winning a game."

While the Pats offense was stagnant, the defense continued to impress. The unit has now allowed just one offensive touchdown over the past four games.

As for Brady, he had his second tough game against the Bills in two outings. Brady (19-of-35, 237 yards, five sacks, one interception) overthrew more receivers in one game than he has all year. He was

out of rhythm and off target much of the day. Brady also nearly had his head knocked off when Clements nailed him in the third quarter and sent his helmet flying.

But Brady stepped up when he had to.

After the Bills' Shayne Graham hit a 41-yard field goal with 5:57 remaining to give the Bills a 9-6 lead, Brady led the Pats on a seven- play, 56-yard drive that resulted in Vinatieri's 25-yard game-tying field goal with 2:50 remaining. Brady was 3-for-4 on the drive.

Like the rest of the Patriots, Brady is now looking to squish the Fish.

"It's obviously our biggest game of the year," said Brady. "They handled us pretty good that first time (a 30-10 Dolphins win Oct. 7). I'm excited to see how we step up when it's really time to step up."

SUPER BOWL CHAMPIONS

" **It's big. Everyone can talk about the playoffs, but the No. 1 goal you set the first day of training camp is winning the AFC East. It's what December football is all about.** "

LAWYER MILLOY

	1st	2nd	3rd	4th	OT	Final
New England	3	3	0	3	3	12
Buffalo	0	0	3	6	0	9

SCORING SUMMARY

Qtr	Team	Play		Time
1st	**PATRIOTS**	FG	Vinatieri 40-yd.	4:02
2nd	**PATRIOTS**	FG	Vinatieri 32-yd.	0:53
3rd	**BILLS**	FG	Graham 41-yd.	11:13
4th	**BILLS**	FG	Graham 25-yd.	10:38
4th	**BILLS**	FG	Graham 41-yd.	5:57
4th	**PATRIOTS**	FG	Vinatieri 25-yd.	2:45
OT	**PATRIOTS**	FG	Vinatieri 23-yd.	9:15

OFFENSE

PATRIOTS

PASSING	ATT	COMP	YDS	INT	TD
Brady	35	19	237	1	0

RECEIVING	ATT	YDS	TD
Patten	3	65	0
Brown	5	62	0
Redmond	3	45	0
Glenn	3	27	0
Wiggins	1	25	0
Pass	1	13	0
Edwards	1	3	0
Faulk	1	2	0
Smith	1	-5	0

RUSHING	ATT	YDS	TD
Smith	20	95	0
Brady	3	13	0
Faulk	2	10	0
Brown	1	9	0
Edwards	1	2	0

BILLS

PASSING	ATT	COMP	YDS	INT	TD
Van Pelt	44	22	219	1	0

RECEIVING	ATT	YDS	TD
Price	4	67	0
Moulds	6	50	0
Riemersma	4	36	0
Centers	2	29	0
Henry	1	14	0
Bryson	3	12	0
Morris	1	8	0
Germany	1	3	0

RUSHING	ATT	YDS	TD
Henry	12	54	0
Bryson	14	38	0
Van Pelt	2	6	0

SUPER BOWL CHAMPIONS

A KICKER'S DREAM

A KICKER'S DREAM

A KICKER'S DREAM

A KICKER'S DREAM

Jim Baker; Boston Herald

Adam Vinatieri has become one of the greatest clutch placekickers in NFL history, and is also proving to be somewhat of a prophet as well.

In fact, Vinatieri envisioned the game-winning 48-yard field goal he converted last night at the Superdome as the game clock ran out, the one that closed out a 20-17 victory over the St. Louis Rams in Super Bowl XXXVI and handed the Patriots the first championship in franchise history.

"I kicked that field goal 1,000 times in my sleep last night," Vinatieri said. "Once it left my foot I was pretty sure it was going through. The guys up front did a great job.

"The beautiful thing about this team is the way it pulls together when nobody but the team members gives us a chance. We've been underdogs all year long. Everybody was writing us off but us."

Vinatieri was asked his thoughts as he watched St. Louis battle back from a 17-3 deficit to tie the game at 17 with 1:30 left in the fourth quarter, and then saw Tom Brady drive the Patriots' offense 53 yards on eight plays to set up the game-winning kick.

"I'll tell you what," said Vinatieri. "I was just so happy the guys moved the ball and gave me an opportunity. It was great. They blocked great up front, the snap and the hold were great. It was unbelievable."

Vinatieri was also asked if he knows Scott Norwood, the former Buffalo Bills kicker who blew a similiar game-winning attempt (a 47-yarder) against the New York Giants in Super Bowl XXV. The Pats soon-to-be free agent kicker said he had never met Norwood but watched that kick while still a high school student in Rapid City, S.D.

When it was pointed out that he hasn't missed a field goal attempt indoors in his six-year career (24-for-24), Vinatieri shrugged off the statistic.

"Matt Bahr always told me you're never as good or as bad as they say you are," said Vinatieri.

The key to the Patriots' late-season and playoff push, a run in which they won their final nine games?

SUPER BOWL CHAMPIONS

"We've been an unbelievably unselfish team," said Vinatieri, "and because of it we're world champions.

"I'm a little hoarse. And that's because I've been screaming a lot. This just hasn't set in yet. It's a total team victory. When you play as a team, there is nothing you can't do."

Vinatieri was asked if this was a bigger kick than either of the two he made in a snowstorm to beat Oakland in the divisional playoffs—but especially the 45-yarder that tied the Raiders and sent the game into overtime.

"That (45-yarder) was tougher, but this is certainly more special," he said.

Vinatieri had been connecting from 59 yards in pregame warmups, but Patriots coach Bill Belichick wanted to move closer.

"We were trying to get one more completion and a few more yards," Belichick said.

Brady coolly dropped back and threw a 6-yarder to Jermaine Wiggins at the 30. Then Brady calmly went to the line and spiked the ball—leaving Vinatieri to walk off the placement for what turned out to be the biggest kick of his, and the team's, life.

The kick was up. The kick was good.

A dream come true for Vinatieri.

FIRST AND FOREMOST,
PATRIOTS SQUISH FISH

Michael Felger; Boston Herald

The Patriots had just taken over first place in the AFC East courtesy of a 20-13 win yesterday over the Miami Dolphins, and coach Bill Belichick was confronted by cameras and microphones as he wandered the field. At that moment, safety Lawyer Milloy came up from behind Belichick and virtually tackled his head coach.

"We're back!" screamed Milloy. "We're back!"

And with that, Belichick led a host of players on a spontaneous, joyous victory lap around Foxboro Stadium, which had just played host to its last regular season game. When the bedlam was complete, Belichick stood in the runway, beaming as his players left the field. Ty Law and Troy Brown ran to the 50-yard line to take a bow.

Now, Patriots fans await the encore.

"I am so thrilled for our football team," said Belichick. "It's a great, emotional day and I'm thrilled to be a part of it."

The feel-good story of the 2001 Patriots added its latest chapter, as the Pats raised their record to 10-5 and put themselves in prime position to return to Foxboro for a playoff game in three weeks.

If the Pats beat Carolina (1-12) in two weeks in Charlotte, N.C., they'll most likely be back at Foxboro the weekend of Jan. 12-13 to host a playoff game. The Patriots would clinch a playoff berth today with a loss by the Jets, Ravens or Seahawks. A win over the Panthers and one more Jets loss would see the Pats crowned division champions.

Not bad for a team that went 5-11 last season and began the 2001 campaign at 1-3. Not bad for a team that was considered too old at many positions, too young at others and not talented enough across the board. It seemed the only people that believed were in the locker room, and yesterday they let that be known.

"A lot of people doubted us," said Pats center Damien Woody. "They've been doubting us all season. It was great to go out and prove people wrong. We were basically running down the (Dolphins') throats and having our way with them. …We're tired of people labeling us and saying we can't do this or we can't do that. The proof is in the pudding."

The Pats pounded the ball on the ground early and often, and while Antowain Smith (156 yards on 26 carries) was outstanding, the offensive line was even better. The Pats ran for 196 yards on the day while the Dolphins could manage just 58 yards.

The Pats also got big games from a group of unsung heroes.

Reserve wide receiver Fred Coleman recovered a Miami fumble off a pooch kick in the first half to set up three points and then came down with an onside kick late in the fourth quarter. Safety Tebucky Jones caused two key fumbles. Reserve fullback Patrick Pass scored his first career touchdown on a 23-yard pass from Tom Brady, with J.R. Redmond and Jermaine Wiggins throwing key blocks to make the play happen.

SUPER BOWL CHAMPIONS

"Every week we're talking about a different player," said Belichick.

The defense was outstanding as usual, holding the Dolphins to one touchdown, that coming in the final two minutes.

The highlight of the day for Brady (11-of-19, 108 yards) came in the first quarter when Kevin Faulk took a direct snap from Mike Compton, rolled right and then lofted a perfect pass to a wide-open Brady in the opposite flat for a 23-yard gain.

"That play hasn't always looked that good in practice—I can tell you that," said Belichick.

The Pats led, 20-3, at the half and weren't seriously threatened until Jeff Ogden came down with a 10-yard touchdown pass from Jay Fielder with 1:28 remaining. A few moments later, it was party time in Foxboro.

Law was asked if the Pats were a Super Bowl team.

"We have the potential to be—but, right now, no," said Law. "When we put things together on offense, defense and special teams, I expect to be in New Orleans. We haven't done that yet. But I wouldn't be surprised if sooner or later I'm down there having some gumbo."

A lot of people doubted us. They've been doubting us all season. It was great to go out and prove people wrong.
PATS CENTER DAMIEN WOODY

	1st	2nd	3rd	4th	Final
Miami	0	3	0	10	13
New England	0	20	0	0	20

SCORING SUMMARY

QTR	TEAM	PLAY		TIME
2nd	**PATRIOTS**	TD	A. Smith 2-yd.run (Vinatieri kick)	14:57
2nd	**PATRIOTS**	TD	Pass 23-yd. pass from Brady (Vinatieri kick)	10:58
2nd	**PATRIOTS**	FG	Vinatieri 32-yd.	4:31
2nd	**PATRIOTS**	FG	Vinatieri 23-yd.	0:57
2nd	**DOLPHINS**	FG	Mare 36-yd.	0:03
4th	**DOLPHINS**	FG	Mare 36-yd.	13:41
4th	**DOLPHINS**	TD	Ogden 10-yd. pass from Fiedler	1:28

OFFENSE

PATRIOTS

PASSING	ATT	COMP	YDS	INT	TD
Brady	19	11	108	0	1
Faulk	1	1	23	0	0

RECEIVING	ATT	YDS	TD
Brown	5	59	0
Pass	2	29	1
Brady	1	23	0
Wiggins	2	8	0
Faulk	1	7	0
Edwards	1	5	0

RUSHING	ATT	YDS	TD
Smith	26	156	1
Redmond	11	35	0
Brown	2	7	0
Edwards	2	3	0
Brady	3	-5	0

DOLPHINS

PASSING	ATT	COMP	YDS	INT	TD
Fiedler	37	21	320	0	1

RECEIVING	ATT	YDS	TD
Chambers	7	124	0
McKnight	5	78	0
Weaver	3	53	0
Ogden	2	28	1
Smith	2	23	0
Konrad	1	7	0
Ward	1	7	0

RUSHING	ATT	YDS	TD
Smith	12	33	0
Fiedler	3	13	0
Minor	3	7	0
Ward	1	5	0

SUPER BOWL CHAMPIONS

PATS PROVE TOP FLIGHT
POUND PANTHERS FOR DIVISION TITLE

Michael Felger; Boston Herald

The infamous "border war" between the Patriots and Jets experienced a rare cease-fire early last evening.

"For the next three hours," said owner Bob Kraft moments after the Pats' AFC East-clinching 38-6 win over the Carolina Panthers, "we're all Jets fans."

The rooting paid off.

While the Pats were cruising at around 35,000 feet aboard their chartered jet bound for Providence, New York Jets kicker John Hall booted a 53-yard field goal with a minute left to beat Oakland, 24-22. Some Patriots personnel had miniature televisions on board the flight and were able to pick up portions of the Jets game. When the game ended, a cheer went through the plane. Thanks to that kick, the Pats head into the playoffs as the second seed in the AFC.

What does that mean? Everything. The Pats now have a bye this weekend (their second in three weeks) and will host a second-round playoff game at Foxboro Stadium the weekend of Jan. 19-20 (opponent to be determined). Incredibly, the Patriots are two wins away from the Super Bowl.

While the Pats will be resting up, they can take pride in an 11-5 record and their first division title in four years. Few observers gave the Pats any chance this season, especially after a 1-3 start and a devastating injury to franchise quarterback Drew Bledsoe in Week 2. But under Coach of the Year candidate Bill Belichick, the Pats rebounded to be the surprise team of the NFL.

"It's a great, great thrill," said Kraft. "The object at the beginning of every year is to make the playoffs. But being in this position after a 1-3 start— it's really satisfying. . . . But it's a whole new season now."

Added Belichick: "Whoever we play, it will be up to us to re-establish our level of play. . . . We're real happy with what we've accomplished. There's a long way to go. We'll enjoy it for a few hours, and then when the seedings come out, we'll set a new target."

The mood in the locker room was one of tempered satisfaction. Belichick got the requisite Gatorade shower and the players left the field pumping their fists. Yet, to a man, the Pats feel they have more victories in them.

Center Damien Woody was asked if the Pats felt they accomplished anything.

"Right there, that's it," said Woody, pointing to his commemorative "AFC East Division Champions" cap. "Right now we can say we're champions of our division. That's a pretty big statement. But it's not over."

Added defensive lineman Bobby Hamilton: "We've set three goals—win the division, win the AFC championship, win the Super Bowl. We've got one of them. Now we're 0-0 when it comes to the second."

The Pats knew that the Raiders were watching the proceedings closely from the West Coast. Linebacker Mike Vrabel said the Pats wanted to put the pressure squarely on Oakland.

SUPER BOWL CHAMPIONS

"It's like putting up a score in golf. Now we sit back and see what the others can do," said Vrabel. "If we keep our heads and don't get too drunk in the clubhouse, we should be just fine when we come back out."

As for the game, the Panthers (six turnovers) were as bad as advertised, and they now own the NFL record for consecutive losses in a season (15). The Pats were able to take advantage, but they didn't play well on either side of the ball. Thankfully for Pats fans, their return game was fantastic, as Otis Smith and Ty Law returned Chris Weinke interceptions for touchdowns and Troy Brown added a 68-yard punt return for a score. Smith had another interception return for a TD called back because of a holding penalty.

Defensively, the Pats were pushed around along the line of scrimmage for the first time in months, and Panthers running back Richard Huntley (168 yards on 22 carries) was made to look like Walter Payton. Offensively, quarterback Tom Brady (17-of-29, 198 yards, one touchdown, two interceptions) was sometimes hot but mostly cold. His two interceptions were uncharacteristically bad decisions in which he threw into coverage.

It was not an encouraging performance from a team that has set its sights on a Super Bowl. But the Patriots, and Brady in particular, have rebounded from poor games all season.

"We're pretty confident," Brady said. "We've been in a lot of situations this year. It's all about controlling our own performance. We control our own attitude, focus and determination. This has been a pretty determined group."

When it was over, the Pats had accomplished what they set out to do. Now they set their sights elsewhere.

"We can't let up," Smith said. "We can't let our game slide at all. We want to play in February. That's our goal."

SUPER BOWL CHAMPIONS

"We're real happy with what we've accomplished. There's a long way to go. We'll enjoy it for a few hours, and then when the seedings come out, we'll set a new target."

PATRIOTS COACH BILL BELICHICK

	1st	2nd	3rd	4th	Final
New England	10	0	14	14	38
Carolina	0	3	3	0	6

SCORING SUMMARY

QTR	TEAM	PLAY		TIME
1st	**PATRIOTS**	FG	Vinatieri 19-yd.	10:04
1st	**PATRIOTS**	TD	Law 46-yd. interception return (Vinatieri kick)	7:58
2nd	**PANTHERS**	FG	Kasay 29-yd.	6:25
3rd	**PATRIOTS**	TD	Brown 68-yd. punt return (Vinatieri kick)	8:30
3rd	**PANTHERS**	FG	Kasay 40-yd.	4:46
3rd	**PATRIOTS**	TD	A. Smith 32-yd. run (Vinatieri kick)	1:29
4th	**PATRIOTS**	TD	Wiggins 5-yd. pass from Brady (Vinatieri kick)	10:38
4th	**PATRIOTS**	TD	O. Smith 76-yd. interception return (Vinatieri kick)	5:45

OFFENSE

PATRIOTS

PASSING	ATT	COMP	YDS	INT	TD
Brady	29	17	198	2	1

RECEIVING	ATT	YDS	TD
Patten	4	54	0
Brown	5	45	0
Redmond	3	42	0
Wiggins	2	36	1
Edwards	1	17	0
Coleman	1	4	0

RUSHING	ATT	YDS	TD
Smith	21	81	1
Redmond	8	15	0
Brown	1	4	0
Edwards	3	3	0
Brady	1	2	0
Faulk	2	-3	0

PANTHERS

PASSING	ATT	COMP	YDS	INT	TD
Weinke	36	15	144	3	0

RECEIVING	ATT	YDS	TD
Hoover	4	44	0
Smith	3	36	0
Huntley	2	23	0
Mangum	3	22	0
Hayes	1	14	0
Jeffers	1	3	0
Goings	1	2	0

RUSHING	ATT	YDS	TD
Huntley	22	168	0
Goings	4	25	0
Weinke	1	0	0

SUPER BOWL CHAMPIONS

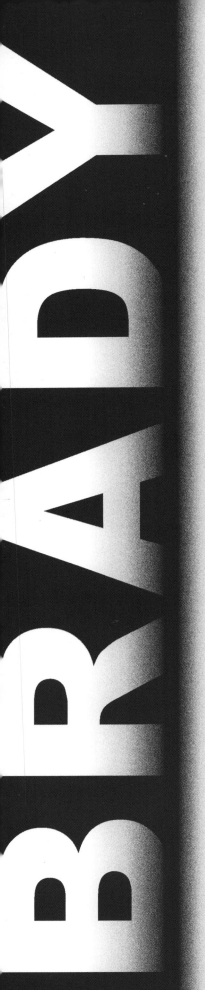

PASSING INTO STARDOM

PASSING INTO STARDOM

PASSING INTO STARDOM

PASSING INTO STARDOM

Mike Gee; Boston Herald

There were 90 seconds to play in Super Bowl XXXVI last night. It was time for Tom Brady's final step from Kid Phenom to Grown-Up Hero.

The Rams just scored a touchdown to tie a game the Pats had won, 17-17. The ball was on the New England 17-yard line and the Pats had no timeouts.

In another life, another time, Brady might've taken a knee and let the Pats take their chances in overtime. For 58:30 of this game, Brady looked every inch a 24-year-old in his first championship game, instructed "for God's sake don't lose it for us." Brady completed 11-of-19 passes for 92 yards to that point, as ordinary as it gets. Tom Brady was ready to seize his time.

"The thought of taking a knee never crossed my mind," Brady said. "I was going to go out and win the game."

Brady's former mentor, Drew Bledsoe, passed the message that the Patriots' torch had passed to Brady for all time.

"Drop back and sling it," Bledsoe told Brady.

Sling it, Tom. This is when quarterbacks win games or lose them. In the final analysis, field generals are measured by what they do the last time their team gets the ball when it needs a score to win.

"That's what's important," Brady said. "To play your best when it's all on the line."

So Brady slung. He slung the way Slingin' Sammy Baugh did, and Otto Graham, Joe Montana, and all the other heroes who've made championship finishes their own.

"That's our team," Brady said. "It's the way we react to the pressure. Everybody steps up."

Brady hit J.R. Redmond three times for 24 yards and two first downs. The Rams blitzed Brady. They forced him into an incompletion. He kept slinging.

Nerves? Brady may not have any. He fell asleep in the Pats' locker room in the interminable wait for the Super Bowl kickoff.

"I hope you enjoyed the pregame show," Brady said. "We all hated it."

As the game mounted into the frenzied chaos of the last 60 seconds, Brady kept his wits about him. No rush. No fuss. He had all the time in the world.

SUPER BOWL CHAMPIONS

"They play kind of a soft zone," Brady said. "We didn't need any touchdown though. Just a 25-yard pass play and we were in position to have Adam (Vinatieri) kick the field goal."

On second-and-10 from the Pats' 41 with 29 seconds left, Brady found that play. It was, as somehow you knew it had to be, to Troy Brown.

"It's 64 Max All In," Brady said. "Max means, blockers, give me more time. The receivers all run in routes. The Ram secondary reads your eyes. I looked right all the way and Troy was able to slide in underneath them to the left."

Brown caught the ball past midfield and slashed down to the St. Louis 36. All of a sudden, the Pats were in field goal range. Brady threw to Jermaine Wiggins for 6 more, let the clock run down to 7 seconds and spiked the ball. He'd completed 5-of-8 passes for 53 yards in 83 seconds.

"That was a pretty well executed two-minute drive," coach Bill Belichick said.

Don't give Brady a swelled head, coach. Vinatieri's field goal could not have been closer to the middle of the uprights. The Patriots were world champions, 20-17.

And Tom Brady was a Phenom no more. He may still look like a kid, but Brady's a Man, the Man, for his football team.

"We seized the opportunity," said the new national hero and Super Bowl MVP.

The MVP completed 16-of-27 passes for 145 yards. Rams quarterback Kurt Warner threw for 365 yards. Go figure.

With quarterbacks, it's not how or even how many. It's when; when championships are there to be won.

DIVISION PLAYOFFS

PATS AWAKEN TO NEW CHALLENGE

Michael Felger; Boston Herald

Like thousands of football fans throughout New England, Bill Belichick slept a little later than usual yesterday morning after spending the previous evening as a witness to the unbelievable.

Unlike those fans, Belichick didn't have the luxury of staying in bed and nursing the hangover from the Patriots' outrageous 16-13 overtime win over the Oakland Raiders at snowbound Foxboro Stadium. Instead, the Pats coach was eventually back at his office, going over film and scouting reports, trying to bring the Pats one step closer to their first NFL championship.

Belichick was able to narrow his focus at around 3:30 p.m., when the Steelers beat Baltimore, 27-10, to set up next Sunday's AFC Championship Game at Heinz Field in Pittsburgh. It will mark the Pats' third trip to the conference finals and first since 1996.

Meanwhile, Foxboro Stadium has officially seen its last game, and it was unlike any other played before it. Work crews will begin demolition today.

"Even though it was a great win for us and really a special game, we've got another one coming up," said Belichick. "I (told the players) to enjoy it but not lose sight of the next target."

That "next target" is the consensus best team in the AFC. The Steelers rolled to the best record in the conference this season on the strength of their ferocious defense, rejuvenated quarterback Kordell Stewart and the power running of "The Bus," running back Jerome Bettis.

Even though Bettis remained on the sidelines yesterday with a groin injury, the Steelers still dominated the defending world champion Ravens. The performance sent a strong message to the Pats that if they play in Pittsburgh the way they played the first three quarters against the Raiders, a trip to the Super Bowl in New Orleans may be out of the question.

Then again, with the way things have gone this season, the Pats could probably get away with anything. They certainly did Saturday night, when a heroic performance by quarterback Tom Brady, a controversial replay reversal and two death-defying Adam Vinatieri field goals overcame nearly 50 minutes of mediocre football.

It was a finish that will be remembered for as long as the Pats play football.

"What can you say?" said special teams captain Larry Izzo, whose recovery of a Troy Brown fumble late in the fourth quarter was just one of many incredible plays. "An ESPN instant classic—right there."

Belichick said he had to scrap around one-third of the game plan because of the conditions. Then at halftime, he and offensive coordinator Charlie Weis made a key adjustment, taking the reins off Brady (32-of-52, 312 yards) and allowing him to speed up the offense and move the ball through the air.

Tight end Jermaine Wiggins was a huge beneficiary, as he caught nine second-half passes.

With Brown drawing double coverage, David Patten also got involved with eight catches for 107 yards on the night.

The Brady non-fumble is the play fans will be talking about for years, but Vinatieri's 45-yard, game-tying field goal off of four inches of snow with 27 seconds left will go down as one of the greatest kicks in team history.

"I'd probably have to say No. 1," said Belichick when asked to rank the biggest kicks he's ever witnessed. "Because of the conditions and what was at stake. That type of kick would be hard in perfect conditions."

Now Belichick, who didn't get home until 2:30 yesterday morning, will try to create some more memories.

"I am sure we will look back on this year and have a lot of special memories," said the coach. "But right now it is really about what is in front of us."

"**What can you say? An ESPN instant classic—right there.**"
SPECIAL TEAMS CAPTAIN LARRY IZZO

PATRIOTS STORM BACK FOR WIN IN OVERTIME

VINATIERI KICK PUTS END TO 16-13 THRILLER

Michael Felger; Boston Herald

The Patriots' magical season blasted head-first through a snow bank and into history last night at Foxboro Stadium.

In one of the most stunning, dramatic games in 42 years of Patriots football, the Pats exorcised the ghost of Ben Dreith and defeated the Oakland Raiders, 16-13, in overtime to advance to next week's AFC Championship Game.

The series of events that led to the victory will go down in Patriots lore. Facing a 10-point, fourth-quarter deficit, the Pats came back on the arm of Tom Brady, a stunning instant replay reversal and two Adam Vinatieri field goals that define the word clutch.

When it was all over, linebacker Tedy Bruschi sat at his locker stall and lied.

"To tell you the truth, I never had a doubt," Bruschi said.

Yeah, right.

Incredibly, unbelievably, the Pats are one win away from the Super Bowl.

"I'm just so happy for our football team and those guys," said coach Bill Belichick, who showed his team a tape of last year's snowbound game in Buffalo to get them prepared for last night. "They just keep fighting. They don't know any other way to do it."

Despite Bruschi's comments, the game was very much in doubt—and when Brady lost the ball on a hit by Charles Woodson with 1:47 remaining and the Raiders recovered, most thought it was over. But referee Walt Coleman reversed the call, ruling that it was an incomplete pass. Five plays later, Vinatieri drove a low, 45-yard field goal just over the crossbar to send the game into overtime. Vinatieri then won the game with a 23-yarder on the first possession of the extra session.

When the game ended, Raiders players chased the officiating crew down the tunnel and Oakland team officials began berating NFL observers in the press box. The call figures to match the controversy created in Oakland 25-plus years ago when referee Dreith called a phantom roughing call on Ray "Sugar Bear" Hamilton in a Pats' postseason loss to the Raiders.

Brady described the disputed fumble this way: "(Woodson) hit me—I wasn't sure. Yeah, I was throwing it. How about that?"

Said Coleman: "When I got over to the replay monitor and looked, it was obvious that his arm was coming forward. He was trying to tuck the ball and they just knocked it out of his hand. His hand was coming forward—which makes it an incomplete pass."

SUPERBOWL CHAMPIONS

Coleman reiterated that if Brady had tucked the ball away after attempting the pass, it would have been a fumble. But Coleman said Brady's arm was still making the throwing motion.

"He has to get it all the way tucked back in order for it to be a fumble," said Coleman."

The second-most incredible play of the night was Vinatieri's game-tying kick. With the Pats out of timeouts, players weren't able to clear the ground for Vinatieri, so he was forced to kick the ball off of about four inches of snow and into a swirling wind. The ball cleared the crossbar by about three feet.

"That's the biggest kick I've ever seen," said Bruschi.

Added Vinatieri: "We were pushing the envelope a little bit."

No kidding. That especially holds true for Brady, who was ineffective in the first half (6-of-13, 74 yards, one interception) only to rebound with a heroic effort in the second half (26-of-39, 238 yards, one rushing TD).

"It's sweet," Brady said. "We just always suck it up when we have to. One way or another, we find a way to win."

> "It's sweet. We just always suck it up when we have to. One way or another, we find a way to win."
> PATRIOTS QUARTERBACK TOM BRADY

	1st	2nd	3rd	4th	OT	Final
Oakland	0	7	6	0	0	13
New England	0	0	3	10	3	16

SCORING SUMMARY

QTR	TEAM	PLAY		TIME
2nd	**RAIDERS**	TD	Jett 13-yd. pass from Gannon (Janikowski kick) ...	12:14
3rd	**PATRIOTS**	FG	Vinatieri 23-yd.	8:39
3rd	**RAIDERS**	FG	Janikowski 38-yd.	4:14
3rd	**RAIDERS**	FG	Janikowski 45-yd.	1:41
4th	**PATRIOTS**	TD	Brady 6-yd. run (Vinatieri kick)	7:52
4th	**PATRIOTS**	FG	Vinatieri 45-yd.	0:27
OT	**PATRIOTS**	FG	Vinatieri 23-yd.	6:31

OFFENSE

PATRIOTS

PASSING	ATT	COMP	YDS	INT	TD
Brady	52	32	312	1	0

RECEIVING	ATT	YDS	TD
Patten	8	107	0
Wiggins	10	68	0
Brown	4	43	0
Redmond	4	43	0
Edwards	3	29	0
Faulk	3	22	0

RUSHING	ATT	YDS	TD
Smith	20	65	0
Brady	5	16	1
Faulk	1	-1	0
Redmond	3	-3	0
Brown	1	-9	0

RAIDERS

PASSING	ATT	COMP	YDS	INT	TD
Gannon	31	17	159	0	1

RECEIVING	ATT	YDS	TD
Rice	4	48	0
Brown	5	42	0
Garner	4	32	0
Jett	2	23	1
Brigham	1	10	0
Porter	1	4	0

RUSHING	ATT	YDS	TD
Garner	17	64	0
Wheatley	4	5	0
Crockett	3	3	0
Kirby	1	3	0
Gannon	5	2	0

CONFERENCE
CHAMPIONSHIP
1.27.02

BAYOU BOUND

Michael Felger; Boston Herald

For the second straight week, instant replay played a key role in a Patriots' playoff game. Unlike last week, however, it didn't come down to just one play.

The Patriots and Steelers used up their allotment of two challenges each in the Pats' 24-17 win in the AFC Championship Game. The replay booth also called for a review during the final two minutes of the first half.

The constant reviewing had referee Ed Hochuli frequently talking to the Heinz Field crowd over his field microphone.

"You can't have more than that," said NFL director of officiating Mike Pereira. "Ed probably has a sore throat."

While it looked like Hochuli could have ruled either way on a few plays—such as an apparent catch by Troy Brown that was overturned in the second quarter—Pereira said Hochuli got the calls right. Pereira also commended Hochuli for frequently going to his mike to explain his rulings.

"He got a lot of air time, sure, but I'd rather he explain everything to the fans than having everyone not know what's going on," Pereira said. "That's what we want our officials to do."

Hochuli reversed an apparent reception by Pittsburgh's Hines Ward in the second quarter.

"He certainly got the incompletions right," Pereira said. "That down by contact call (on an apparent Ward fumble in the third quarter) was a close one. I'll have to take a closer look at them (today)."

Drew Bledsoe left the field arm-in-arm with his father Mac, who was later seen clutching a game ball saved by Bledsoe.

"We have a phrase in the family: It's the Bledsoes against the world," said Mac Bledsoe. "(Drew) told me that that one was for us."

Mac Bledsoe has traveled to the last few games even though his son wasn't playing.

"We just wanted to show that this game is more than just scoring touchdowns and all that," Mac Bledsoe said. "It's no different than all season long. The place where it takes courage and fortitude is when the going is tough. Once you get on the field, that's the (easy) part."

When Drew Bledsoe passed Tom Brady in the locker room after the game, he looked down at Brady's left foot and saw only Brady's shoe covering his injured ankle.

"You going to get some ice on that, dude?" Bledsoe said. "The thing is going to blow up like a basketball."

Offensive coordinator Charlie Weis said he didn't change the playbook when Bledsoe entered the game. Weis said the plan was to stay aggressive no matter who the quarterback was.

"We just called the next play," Weis said. "This kid's been a good quarterback for a long time. We couldn't play the game to lose. We had to play the game to win. . . . The moment he entered the game is the time he feels the most comfortable, in the no-huddle. We did not change a thing. The only thing I did was, at halftime, I went to him and said, 'Do you want to go with anything?' And he just said, 'You call 'em and I wing 'em.'"

SUPER BOWL CHAMPIONS

Meanwhile, some players were wondering whether Weis would be able to coach the team this week given the fact his contract is set to expire on Friday. Since the league pushed the schedule back a week after the Sept. 11 terrorist attacks, Weis will be covered until after the Super Bowl.

As planned, the widow of former quarterbacks coach Dick Rehbein, Pam, and her two daughters, Betsy and Sarabeth, represented the Pats in the pregame coin flip. "The players genuinely feel his presence," said owner Robert Kraft of Dick Rehbein. "I believe they thought he was their good-luck charm. Everything seems to come together in strange ways."

Yesterday marked the two-year anniversary of the Pats' hiring of Bill Belichick as head coach. Kraft had to give the New York Jets a first-round pick to pry Belichick out of his contract.

"It was the cheapest deal I've ever done," said Kraft, who spoke to the team in the locker room.

SUPER BOWL CHAMPIONS

"This kid's been a good quarterback for a long time. We couldn't play the game to lose. We had to play the game to win."

OFFENSIVE COORDINATOR CHARLIE WEIS

CONFERENCE
CHAMPIONSHIP

BELICHICK MAKES HIS POINTS

Mark Murphy; Boston Herald

Never let them tell you that coaches don't follow the line.

Patriots coach Bill Belichick took the 9 1/2 points the Steelers were favored by—and the slight they represented—and whipped himself and his team into an indignant fury last week.

Roughly 30 minutes after the Patriots made good on that anger yesterday with a 24-17 win over Pittsburgh in the AFC Championship Game at Heinz Field, the coach blurted out the secret.

"We don't care (about being underrated)," he said, an expression of disgust replacing the usual deadpan. "The spread was the same for us as when Pittsburgh played 1-12 Detroit a couple of weeks ago. The big thing is being ready to play."

That last statement may sound absurdly simple, but now that Belichick is taking the Patriots to the Super Bowl for the first time as a head coach, it is also gospel.

Yesterday's result offered further proof. In his time as a defensive coordinator and head coach, Belichick has scrambled the thoughts of many good quarterbacks, including Peyton Manning, Doug Flutie and even Drew Bledsoe.

Yesterday, his defense brought a sizzling Kordell Stewart back to earth.

"(Belichick) comes up with such a strong game plan, and if you believe in that, you will beat anyone," said defensive end Bobby Hamilton. "He will always be ready, and he will always have his team ready."

Said rookie tackle Richard Seymour: "It's preparation with him. He puts you in the position to make those plays."

This season, however, that challenge went far beyond game preparation. From his handling of the recalcitrant Terry Glenn to picking a starting quarterback—an issue that was revisited yesterday thanks to Tom Brady's leg injury—Belichick managed to live with and survive by his decisions.

"We totally believe in him," Seymour said. "If he tells us to do something, you'd better believe we're going to do it."

By the time he reached the postgame podium, Belichick looked like a man who had just walked through a wind tunnel. His jacket, hat and the hair underneath it were all askew.

Asked to think back over this wild season, he let out an exasperated sigh. It was truly all a blur.

"Just that the guys who believe in this team are the ones standing in that locker room," he said. "We've been through a lot of things, but those guys keep believing in each other."

SUPER BOWL CHAMPIONS

"Just that the guys who believe in this team are the ones standing in that locker room. We've been through a lot of things, but those guys keep believing in each other."

PATRIOTS COACH BILL BELICHICK

	1st	2nd	3rd	4th	Final
New England	7	7	7	3	24
Pittsburgh	0	3	14	0	17

SCORING SUMMARY

Qtr	Team	Play		Time
1st	**PATRIOTS**	TD	Brown 55-yd. punt return (Vinatieri kick)	3:42
2nd	**STEELERS**	FG	Brown 30-yd.	13:33
2nd	**PATRIOTS**	TD	Patten 11-yd. pass from Bledsoe (Vinatieri kick)	0:58
3rd	**PATRIOTS**	TD	Harris 49-yd. blocked FG return (Vinatieri kick) ...	8:51
3rd	**STEELERS**	TD	Bettis 1-yd. run (Brown kick)	5:11
3rd	**STEELERS**	TD	Zereoue 11-yd. run (Brown kick)	1:29
4th	**PATRIOTS**	FG	Vinatieri 44-yd.	11:12

OFFENSE

PATRIOTS

PASSING	ATT	COMP	YDS	INT	TD
Brady	18	12	115	0	0
Bledsoe	21	10	102	0	1

RECEIVING	ATT	YDS	TD
Brown	8	121	0
Patten	4	39	1
Edwards	4	26	0
Johnson	2	22	0
Wiggins	2	7	0
Redmond	2	2	0

RUSHING	ATT	YDS	TD
Smith	15	47	0
Redmond	3	13	0
Brady	2	3	0
Edwards	1	3	0
Bledsoe	4	1	0

STEELERS

PASSING	ATT	COMP	YDS	INT	TD
Stewart	42	24	255	3	0

RECEIVING	ATT	YDS	TD
Burress	5	67	0
Ward	6	64	0
Zereoue	4	50	0
Bettis	2	23	0
Edwards	2	16	0
Kreider	2	13	0
Cushing	1	10	0
Shaw	1	9	0
Tuman	1	3	0

RUSHING	ATT	YDS	TD
Stewart	8	41	0
Zereoue	4	11	1
Bettis	9	8	1
Ward	1	-2	0

SUPER BOWL CHAMPIONS

SUPER ENDING FOR PATS
VINATIERI CLINCHES TITLE ON FINAL PLAY

Michael Felger; Boston Herald

Do you believe in miracles? The Patriots don't. Adam Vinatieri doesn't. The Patriots believe in themselves.

And now so does everybody else.

In a heart-stopping, gut-wrenching performance that shocked the football world and will go down in the annals of pro sports, the Patriots upset the St. Louis Rams in Super Bowl XXXVI, 20-17, and claimed their first NFL title last night.

Vinatieri was the hero, as he booted a 48-yard field goal as time expired to give Boston its first pro championship in 16 years.

"The fans of New England have been waiting 42 years for this," said owner Bob Kraft. "We're the champs!"

Vinatieri's kick culminated an ultra-clutch, nine-play, 53-yard drive by Tom Brady and the offense after the Rams had tied the game with 1:30 left on a Ricky Proehl 26-yard touchdown catch.

The game was supposed to be about the high-flying Rams offense; instead, it was another showcase for the gritty, hard-hitting Patriots and the uncanny defensive schemes of coach Bill Belichick.

It all added up to an incredible night of football, one that allowed fans throughout New England to sit back this morning and savor a magical moment.

Say these words slowly:

New England Patriots—world champions.

Was it the greatest night in the history of Boston sports? How could it not be? It was surely the biggest night in the 42 years of Patriots football. And

the formula was the same as it's been all season: clutch defense, opportunistic offense and out-of-this world coaching from Belichick.

Brady, the youngest quarterback ever win a Super Bowl, took a pregame pain injection for his sprained left ankle, but he showed few effects of the injury. He completed 16-of-27 passes for 145 yards and had a beautiful 8-yard scoring strike to David Patten just before halftime.

The defense did its usual stellar work, remarkably holding the Rams to two touchdowns. The key plays were an interception return for a touchdown from Ty Law and a fumble recovery by Terrell Buckley in the first half, and an Otis Smith interception in the second half.

The Pats took a stunning 14-3 lead into the half. When the Pats emerged for the second half, Belichick still had his poker face on. "We're just going to have to keep doing it," said the coach.

The second half featured a heart-breaking play for the Pats. With the Rams facing fourth-and-goal from the 3-yard line, Roman Phifer stripped Kurt Warner of the ball and Tebucky Jones picked it up and raced 98 yards for an apparent touchdown. But Willie McGinest was flagged for holding Marshall Faulk on the play, and the Rams got a fresh set of downs.

Two plays later Warner scored from 2 yards out to bring the Rams to within a touchdown.

McGinest later got his redemption, sacking Warner with just over four minutes left to help kill a Rams drive.

The game started as so many others have for the Pats, with the team eschewing individual introductions during the pregame warmups and coming onto the field as one. The entire team also came out near midfield for the coin toss, which was won by the Rams (heads).

The Pats then weathered the Rams' opening flurry. After Yo Murphy returned the opening kickoff to the Rams' 39, Warner hit Torry Holt for an 18-yard gain on second down. But the Rams could do no more damage, as an offensive interference call put them back. Punter John Baker pinned the Pats on their own 3-yard line.

The Pats' offense was crisp to open, as Brady hit Troy Brown with a 21-yard slant pattern over the middle on first down. Antowain Smith then gained 9 yards on a sweep on the next play, and Brady

followed that up with a 10-yard gain to Brown. The drive later stalled, but not before Brady's sprained left ankle was put to the test when he was hit on a scramble down the left sideline. Brady got right up and ran off the field, showing no ill-effects from the hit.

The Rams got on the board first, as Jeff Wilkins hit a 48-yard field goal with 3:10 left in the first quarter. Wilkins later had a chance to increase the lead, but he missed wide left from 52 yards out.

The Pats went ahead with 8:49 remaining in the first half on Law's interception return. On the play, linebacker Mike Vrabel applied pressure on Warner (avoiding a roughing penalty after hitting Warner in the head) and Law was there to pick off the sloppy pass. He went untouched down the left sideline.

SUPER BOWL CHAMPIONS

The fans of New England have been waiting 42 years for this. We're the champs!

PATRIOTS OWNER BOB KRAFT

SUPER BOWL CHAMPIONS

BROWN STEPS ON THE CLUTCH
TROY STEERS CLEAR ON PATS' CRITICAL DRIVE

Michael Felger; Boston Herald

When the chips were down throughout the season, the Patriots called on Troy Brown to bail them out.

Last night was another case of the wide receiver to the rescue.

After the Rams rallied with two late touchdowns to tie the score at 17 with 1:30 left, Brown slipped into his Superman's cape and helped deliver the first Super Bowl triumph to the Patriots.

On a second-and-10 from the Pats' 41-yard line, Brown slipped free over the middle, caught a pass from Tom Brady and raced 23 yards to the Rams' 36. Three plays later, Adam Vinatieri's 48-yard field goal gave the Pats a stunning 20-17 victory in Super Bowl XXXVI.

"They were in a zone defense and I saw the linebacker dropping deep," said Brown, who finished with six catches for 89 yards. "On the other side of me was the dead spot of the zone, so I knew I had to get over there to have a chance to get it. Tom did a good job of stepping up and finding me. He hit me with a good pass over the middle and I was able to get out of bounds at the same time."

Some questioned whether it was prudent for the Pats to throw the ball from deep in their own territory in the final minute of regulation. Brown wasn't among them.

"We play the whole 60 minutes—that's what we do around here," said Brown. "We've said that all year—you learn to play the entire game. Tom did a great job of moving us down the field, hitting the open guys, checkdowns, whatever. That last drive was tremendous for him."

Brown never saw the game-winning kick. Having turned in the other direction when Vinatieri made his clutch kicks against the Oakland Raiders in the AFC divisional win, Brown wasn't about to tempt fate.

"I didn't watch the kick," Brown said. "But I saw the guys behind me jumping up and down when he hit it, so I knew it was good. It was time to party after that."

Forget about winning the Super Bowl—just stepping on the field put Brown a leg up on 1997. The wide receiver/special teams ace was a scratch (hernia) from the Super Bowl XXXI loss against the Green Bay Packers.

"It's a tremendous feeling right now," said Brown, who will head to Honolulu for the Pro Bowl this Saturday. "The first time I missed it and we lost. This time I got a chance to play and we ended up winning. This is what I've dreamed about my whole life, being a little boy growing up, playing in a Super Bowl and winning it. And here we are, Super Bowl champs."

"This is what I've dreamed about my whole life, being a little boy growing up, playing in a Super Bowl and winning it. And here we are, Super Bowl champs."

PATRIOTS WIDE RECEIVER TROY BROWN

SUPER BOWL CHAMPIONS

**"Say these words slowly:
New England Patriots—world champions."**

SUPER BOWL CHAMPIONS

	1st	2nd	3rd	4th	Final
St. Louis	3	0	0	14	17
New England	0	14	3	3	20

SCORING SUMMARY

Qtr	Team	Play	Time
1st	**RAMS**	FG Wilkins 50-yd.	3:10
2nd	**PATRIOTS**	TD Law 47-yd. interception return (Vinatieri kick)	8:49
2nd	**PATRIOTS**	TD Patten 8-yd. pass from Brady (Vinatieri kick)	0:31
3rd	**PATRIOTS**	FG Vinatieri 37-yd.	1:18
4th	**RAMS**	TD Warner 2-yd. run (Wilkins kick)	9:31
4th	**RAMS**	TD Proehl 26-yd. pass from Warner (Wilkins kick)	1:30
4th	**PATRIOTS**	FG Vinatieri 48-yd.	0:00

OFFENSE

PATRIOTS

PASSING	ATT	COMP	YDS	INT	TD
Brady	27	16	145	0	1

RECEIVING	ATT	YDS	TD
Brown	6	89	0
Redmond	3	24	0
Wiggins	2	14	0
Patten	1	8	1
Edwards	2	7	0
Smith	1	4	0
Faulk	1	-1	0

RUSHING	ATT	YDS	TD
Smith	18	92	0
Patten	1	22	0
Faulk	2	15	0
Edwards	2	5	0
Brady	1	3	0
Redmond	1	-4	0

RAMS

PASSING	ATT	COMP	YDS	INT	TD
Warner	44	28	365	2	1

RECEIVING	ATT	YDS	TD
Hakim	5	90	0
Proehl	3	71	1
Bruce	5	56	0
Faulk	4	54	0
Holt	5	49	0
Robinson	2	18	0
Murphy	1	11	0
Conwell	2	8	0
Hodgins	1	8	0

RUSHING	ATT	YDS	TD
Faulk	17	76	0
Warner	3	6	1
Hakim	1	5	0
Hodgins	1	3	0

SUPER BOWL CHAMPIONS

PATRIOTS' REGULAR-SEASON STATISTICS

OFFENSE

PASSING

PLAYER	ATT	CMP	PCT	YDS	TD	INT
Brady	413	264	63.9	2843	18	12
Bledsoe	66	40	60.6	400	2	2
Patten	2	1	50.0	60	1	1
Faulk	1	1	100.0	23	0	0

RECEIVING

PLAYER	ATT	YDS	AVG	TD
Brown	101	1199	11.9	5
Patten	51	749	14.7	4
Glenn	14	204	14.6	1
A. Smith	19	192	10.1	1
Faulk	30	189	6.3	2
Edwards	25	166	6.6	2
Wiggins	14	133	9.5	4
Redmond	13	132	10.2	0
Johnson	14	111	7.9	1
Pass	6	66	11.0	1
Coleman	2	50	25.0	0
Rutledge	5	35	7.0	0
Small	4	29	7.3	0
Emanuel	4	25	6.3	0
Brady	1	23	23.0	0
Jackson	2	16	8.0	0
Cox	1	7	7.0	0

RUSHING

PLAYER	ATT	YDS	AVG	TD
A. Smith	287	1157	4.0	12
Faulk	41	169	4.1	1
Edwards	51	141	2.8	1
Redmond	35	119	3.4	0
Brown	11	91	8.3	0
Patten	5	67	13.4	1
Brady	36	43	1.2	0
Bledsoe	5	18	3.6	0
Pass	1	7	7.0	0
Johnson	1	-19	-19.0	0

SPECIAL TEAMS

FIELD GOALS

PLAYER	1-19	20-29	30-39	40-49	50+
Vinatieri	1/1	8/8	7/8	7/12	1/1

PUNTING

PLAYER	NO	AVG	INSIDE 20
Walter	49	40.1	24
L. Johnson	24	43.5	3
Vinatieri	1	33.0	1

PUNT RETURNS

PLAYER	NO	FC	YDS	AVG	TD
Brown	29	15	413	14.2	2
Faulk	4	0	27	6.8	0

KICKOFF RETURNS

PLAYER	NO	YDS	AVG	TD
Faulk	33	662	20.1	0
Pass	10	222	22.2	0
Kelly	7	123	17.6	0
Redmond	2	57	28.5	0
Patten	2	44	22.0	0
Jackson	2	30	15.0	0
Edwards	1	23	23.0	0
Brown	1	13	13.0	0
Bruschi	1	10	10.0	0

DEFENSE

TACKLES

PLAYER	NO	SOLO	AST
Milloy	77	58	36
Phifer	70	52	21
Law	59	42	10
O. Smith	55	43	8
Bruschi	54	30	21
T. Jones	50	38	19
Vrabel	40	32	23
Pleasant	35	20	8

PLAYER	NO	SOLO	AST	PLAYER	NO	SOLO	AST
Cox	34	19	15	Harris	4	3	3
T. Johnson	32	17	13	Brown	3	3	0
Hamilton	31	16	21	Vinatieri	3	3	1
Stevens	30	23	13	Brady	3	3	0
Buckley	26	20	2	Redmond	3	2	1
Mitchell	26	16	17	Nugent	3	1	1
Seymour	25	15	19	Coleman	2	1	0
McGinest	24	19	8	Edwards	2	2	1
Shaw	23	17	3	Wiggins	2	2	0
Izzo	15	11	8	Faulk	1	1	0
Chatham	13	8	1	Andruzzi	1	1	0
Cherry	11	9	4	Patten	1	1	0
Pass	9	4	2	Paxton	1	1	0
Parker	7	6	3	C. Johnson	1	1	0
Myers	5	4	2				

SACKS

PLAYER	NO		PLAYER	NO
Milloy	3		Pleasant	6
Phifer	2		Hamilton	7
Law	1		Buckley	1
O. Smith	2		Mitchell	1
Bruschi	2		Seymour	3
T. Jones	1		McGinest	5
Vrabel	3		Parker	1

INTERCEPTIONS

Player	No	Yds	Avg	TD
O. Smith	5	181	36.2	2
Law	3	91	30.3	2
Buckley	3	76	25.3	1
Vrabel	2	27	13.5	0
Pleasant	2	0	0.0	0
Milloy	2	21	10.5	0
Bruschi	2	7	3.5	0
Stevens	1	9	9.0	0
T. Jones	1	-4	-4.0	0
Phifer	1	14	14.0	0

TEAM

	PATRIOTS	OPP
Total 1st downs	292	303
Rushing	101	99
Passing	163	171
3rd down: made/att	91/221	80/215
Net yards rushing	1793	1855
Net yards passing	3089	3497
Sacks	40	46
Touchdowns	43	26
Rushing	15	7
Passing	21	15

The entire staff of the *Boston Herald* Photography
Department contributed to the coverage of the New England Patriots'
2001-2002 season, which culminated in a Super Bowl victory.
We gratefully acknowledge the efforts of:

Mike Adaskaveg
Tara Bricking
John Cummings
Renee Dekona
Robert Eng
Michael Fein
Ted Fitzgerald
Mark Garfinkel
David Goldman
Jon Hill
Nancy Lane
Jim Mahoney
George Martell
Ren Norton
Michael Seamans
Matt Stone
Kuni Takahashi
Matthew West
Patrick Whittemore
John Wilcox
Kevin Wisniewski
Darlene Sarno, Technical Support

John Landers, Chief Photographer
Ted Ancher, Assistant Director of Photography
Arthur Pollock, Assistant Director of Photography
Garo Lachinian, Director of Photography